ABUNDANCE

AND

PROSPERITY

A PRACTICAL APPROACH

BY LIZ ADAMSON

ABUNDANCE AND PROSPERITY.
A Practical Approach

by Liz Adamson

Published by Diviniti Publishing Ltd
83, Birling Rd, Leybourne, Kent ME19 5HZ
Tel: 01732 220373
Email admin@hypnosisaudio.com
Website: www.hypnosisaudio.com

ISBN 1 901923 40 1

1st Edition

Cover image by Diane Frost

INTRODUCTION

I felt the need to write this book because lack of abundance seemed to be an issue that was detrimentally affecting many of my clients. While everyone was making huge strides in other areas of life this particular one seemed to be eluding everyone, myself included.

When I began to look into the subject I realised how complex it actually is. There are so many factors that play a part in determining our abundance and many of these seem to be totally conflicting. It's no wonder we become confused by all the different messages we receive. This process, therefore, involves a good deal of weeding and discarding.

Writing this book has been a wonderful experience for me. Since the information has not come from me but through me, it has been very easy, more like taking dictation and much of the information has been a revelation to me as it manifested itself on the page.

I really believe that the time has come to step out of our cycles of struggle, survival and lack. We want to have our own source of abundance without having to depend on others or our employers just in order to survive. We are all meant to be prosperous. We do not need to do anything to deserve this prosperity, it is there ready and waiting for us to claim it. The problem is that most of us do not know that it is there, let alone that we have any rights to it.

I have to say that this is an active and not a passive process. I would suggest that you read through the book once before you start doing the exercises and visualisations. I would also recommend that, if at all possible, you work with a partner or a group. This is not essential but often things become much clearer with discussion and feedback. It also makes it a much more enjoyable process and joy is an important ingredient in abundance. Try not to do too much too quickly as this might lead to a sense of being overwhelmed. Also, there does need to be a period of integration after any piece of work.

The only things you need to do this process are an open mind and a willingness to create your highest good. Ask for help and guidance and let go of all expectations.

GOOD LUCK

I wish you all an abundant life.

Liz Adamson

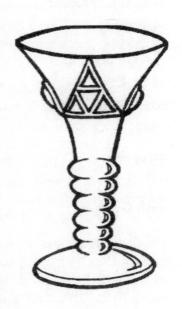

ORDER

THE NEW APPROACH TO PROSPERITY

This plan is not a get rich quick book such as those that were popular in the Seventies and Eighties. These were mainly from America and involved using positive thought and motivation to increase sales quotas. They chiefly involved the business work place. Since then we have had recessions, mass redundancy and negative equity. There is no such thing as a job for life anymore and the legacy of this is a great deal of fear and insecurity. The old order is crumbling; this is an inevitable process for it is making way for the new order. We are in the middle of that transition at this time and the world seems to be chaotic. Many of the large institutions are showing that their foundations are on very shaky ground. The monarchy, banks, the judicial system, insurance companies, marriage, all these have had a rough ride over recent years.

The human condition will always resist change, even if that change is for the better. It will cling to what is familiar even when it is negative and abusive. Think how many people over fifty had to be dragged kicking and screaming into the computer age and now wonder how they ever managed without it.

The masculine principle involves using the intellect, the logical left side of the brain, using strength and domination. It has a strong need to protect what it perceives as owning while at the same time it wants to expand and improve upon what it has. It has a need to be in control in order to have a feeling of security. It has an earth based approach to life. It sees the earth and what it has to offer as the total sum of available prosperity. Therefore, there is a need to acquire it before someone else does and makes it unavailable. This is the way that governments have been working.

The female principle is involved more with nurturing and uses the right side of the brain. It is more intuitive and creative and sees its scope as being far larger than what is on the material or physical. It also has the need to protect anyone or anything that is unable to take care of itself. It is perfectly willing to accept guidance from and give over control to a higher source.

For thousands of years now the world has been working on the masculine principle but that clearly has not worked. It has reached the stage where we have all but destroyed the planet, where wars and famine abound. The pendulum is now swinging the other way and it is the female principle that is going to usher in the new order. I daresay there will be a time of adjustment where it will seem as if the pendulum has swung too far before we come into a balance of male and female.

I am not referring here to men and women but to male and female energy in all of us regardless of sex. More of this later.

The old order was very focused on money, the material and acquisitiveness. Just look at the "American Dream" whereby each person could own their own home and all the trappings and have a high standard of living. The desire to create and keep this has turned into a nightmare for some. For those who have achieved this so called dream, it has not fulfilled the expectations. They still feel empty inside and many have turned to drugs, alcohol and sex to try and alleviate this. Others believe that they don't feel good because they don't have enough and therefore strive to acquire more and more. For those who do not achieve the dream, some also turn to drink, drugs, sex or food to blot out their sense of failure while others work harder or take on more jobs trying to keep up and others still spend their time stealing from those who appear to have it. This system clearly does not work since the emphasis is put on what we have and not who we are inside.

The new order focuses on abundance, fulfilment, love, peace and harmony. These are qualities that virtually everyone would profess to want and yet very few people are making the choices necessary to obtain them. These choices are: deciding only to have beliefs and thoughts which promote the manifestation of these qualities; letting go the fears that block them; opening up on a spiritual level whereby we can tap into our intuition and guidance in any given moment; taking control from the ego and giving it to the higher self; TRUSTING that everything is taken care of and loving ourselves enough to allow all of the above. Learning how to make these choices is the intention of this book since most of us will not be consciously aware of not doing these things.

The challenge we are facing now is that we will be going against the vast majority of world thinking. It will seem as if we are swimming against the tide of negative thought and fear. Friends and family may accuse us of being idealistic, unrealistic and stupid. We can not allow ourselves to be discouraged by any ridicule we may receive. We are spearheading a new way of being that can be common place in as little as ten years. Many people can only be convinced by what they can see, hear and touch. When our change of fortune becomes apparent, others will want to know the whys and wherefores. In the past we have always gone along with seeing is believing. Now the opposite is true. "Believing is seeing." We create what we believe.

There is more than enough abundance for every person on this planet and yet probably more than 95% of the population see this as being out of their reach. This is either because they do not believe in its existence, or because they are not able or willing to do what the old order proclaims they need to in order to get it. Imagine transporting famine victims from Africa to a western supermarket, they would not believe that such bounty could exist. Equally, we cannot even imagine the abundance that lies in store for us if we are only willing to embrace it.

The most important thing is that we stop believing that our only source of abundance is the finite money and resources on this planet which we have all but drained dry and see that the real source is the infinite well of abundance in the Universe that we can tap into at any time.

The time has come to let go of the old order and welcome the changes that are ushering in the new.

EXERCISES

1) Have a willingness to see things in a different way.
2) Affirm to yourself that you are willing to make the necessary changes in your perception in order to bring in the new order of abundance into your life.

ABUNDANCE AND MONEY

In this plan I would like to take the main focus of attention away from money alone and put it more onto the bigger picture of abundance.

There is so much emotional, mental and spiritual baggage put onto money that we have totally lost sight of what it is in its true essence. Physically it is just paper or metal with writing and pictures on. It is merely something that is used in exchange for goods and services.

If we ask someone what they think money is they will usually give us their emotional response to it or judgements about it. For instance, "Money corrupts" or "I love money and wish I had more of it". Money is such an emotive subject that very few people can view it dispassionately. Some people are quite hostile to it because they see money as being the source of most of their problems, therefore they focus their frustration on the money rather than looking for the real problem. Others focus on their love of money because they see money as being the thing that makes them successful and acceptable to others and therefore covers up their own insecurity.

We all have negative and positive statements about money. "Money is the root of all evil." "Where there is muck there is brass." "Money corrupts" or "I love money". "If I had enough money my life would be perfect." Money is just an energy; it is neither negative or positive. It is the scapegoat for many of our feelings and insecurities and has got buried under all the baggage that we have put upon it.

While we live in the present system, money is what we use to buy what we need and in our society we cannot do without it. We have to buy shelter, warmth, food, clothing and many other necessities. There is no way in the western world that we can withdraw from the money system and become totally self-sufficient. It is pointless trying to deny it or pretend we don't need it. Denying money will block abundance. It is like trying to deny that we need the air that we breathe. Equally, greed or the need to acquire more and more in order to feel powerful or in control or whatever, will block abundance.

Money does not buy freedom, security, happiness or love. However, when we tap into those qualities inside us then money or the means to manifest them in the physical will appear. Money is the effect not the cause.

So let us turn our attention to abundance. The dictionary says it is "An extremely plentiful or over sufficient supply". My personal definition is "having more than enough for all our needs wants and desires." To many people abundance conjures up a picture of an utopian society or a Garden of Eden where everything we could need or want abounds. This seems so far removed from our present existence on the Earth that it is hard to believe that we can get from here to there. All that is required is a change of perception. The Garden of Eden is here. Heaven is on Earth and so is Hell. It all depends on which we choose to see.

Therefore, if we focus our attention on scarcity and lack then that is what we are giving our energy to and the energy will expand the scarcity and lack. Even if we are not yet at the stage where we can completely embrace the concept of abundance, it is important to make an effort not to think about what we don't have, what we can't afford and whether we are going to have enough to pay the bills. Instead, we can put the focus on what we do have.

In 'Mutant Message Down Under', Marlo Morgan tells how she walked across central Australia with an aboriginal tribe. They travelled through the hottest and most arid desert imaginable carrying only a dingo skin to lie on and a bottle made from an animal bladder to carry water. Every morning they would stand to the east and thank the Universe for the abundance the Source was going to give them that day and every day. When the time came to eat some food would present itself. Not a hamburger and chips perhaps but enough to sustain them. These people are truly abundant in a land which to our perception is not. It is their total trust that all their needs would be provided for that created that reality.

When we focus our attention on money there never seems to be enough. Billionaires spend their time trying to make more. The more money we have, the more we end up paying out. Each time we move into a higher money bracket, we probably have a bigger house that requires more maintenance and costs a great deal more to run. We probably need to have staff to help us and they require wages. At the end of the day we would probably not feel any better off than when we had a much simpler existence. We know we are truly abundant when we don't have to give a thought to the whys and wherefores but just accept that it is there.

Abundance also covers a much broader area. It involves friendship, love, laughter, joy, beauty, nature, creative fulfilment, good health and happiness. Most people spend at least a third of their adult life working in order to get enough money just to survive, leaving very little time or energy for all the above qualities. If that time is spent doing a job we don't enjoy then there is something very wrong with the system. Our time on Earth was not designed to be totally taken up with survival. We have created this reality by buying into the fear and negativity. The Earth is an abundant playground where we are meant to learn and grow. Just as we have created the hell we can also create the Heaven. One of my favourite quotes is from Maya Angelou: "The purpose of my life is not just to survive but to thrive with passion, compassion, humour and style".

In our present society we measure success by a person's apparent wealth. If someone drives by in a fancy new car we think, "They must be doing all right." The fact that that car is in reality owned by the bank is neither here nor there. If all money were wiped out tomorrow those people with gifts and creative talents would become the successful ones.

The LET scheme has been set up to bring back bartering, swapping goods or services with others within the group. However, since the people we are bartering with may not want our particular goods or services, there is a system of credits, in one group pebbles are used. Each group has its own name for each credit. In Guildford it is Guilds, in Dorking it is Dorks. In effect money has been replaced by pebbles. Imagine if this became universal, our worth would be measured by how many pebbles we have in the bank.

By doing this plan I would certainly expect there to be an increase in income but I would ask that we put money in perspective and not to focus and fixate on the money so much as the part it plays in the bigger picture. It is just the medium of exchange, no different from a pebble really. It is our abundance we are looking to increase on every level.

EXERCISES

1) What does money mean to you?

2) What does abundance mean to you?

3) When you write your ideas of what money means check out how much of this is a judgement on money or an emotional response to it. If this is the case it is something you need to look at and let go of. Money is just an energy used in exchange for goods and services. It needs to be seen for what it is and not as all the things we put onto it.

4) With abundance, check out if it is something you believe that it is available to you, or just as a pie in the sky concept that doesn't exist.

YOU CANNOT HAVE ABUNDANCE IF YOU DON'T BELIEVE IT EXISTS.

RESISTANCE & APATHY

SURRENDER IS THE KEY TO LETTING GO
RESISTANCE

There is a great deal of apathy and resistance that comes up when looking at abundance. In my groups I noticed that almost everybody, myself included, were very nearly asleep when looking at the mental blocks to abundance. This was not totally because I was being very boring at the time. This is such a huge issue, there is an urge to go unconscious. It is a very big subject to tackle and in order to see a shift we have to change deeply embedded belief systems, not just our own beliefs but those of society. It may feel like we will be swimming against the tide of popular thinking and it seems that the energy needed to do this would be monumental. This is the illusion not the reality. It takes no more energy to hold one belief that it does another.

Resistance is created when one force meets another force. the result is stalemate. It is like two lorries travelling in opposite directions down a country lane, when they meet neither driver will back up to allow the other one by. Resistance occurs for us when an idea is put forward to be implemented in our lives. This idea is usually something that would be of benefit to us, like getting fit, finding a better job or bringing abundance into our lives. The ego mind immediately sets up an equal and opposite force that blocks the change taking place. If this resistance is strong then it takes a great deal of energy to push through it and most people give up defeated. We then give ourselves a very hard time for not being able to make this beneficial change and will often do some self-punishing behaviour that compounds our feelings of self loathing. So we have a vicious cycle here.

The answer to dealing with resistance is to surrender. We are taught in our macho society that to surrender is to lose. The reality is very different. Suppose one or other side had surrendered a few days after the outbreak of the First World War, millions of lives on either side would have been saved. This would be a win in my book. Going back to the two lorries stuck in the country lane, if one backed up and allowed the other to pass then both would be able to get on their way, surely this is an improvement on being stuck, even if we were the one to give way.

Those of us who have a stubborn streak (myself included) will tend to have the greatest resistance. Often this stubbornness will have been created in childhood as a response to perhaps some abuse or strict parenting and from this point of view it is positive. It has allowed the person to survive and keep a sense of self under difficult circumstances. However, we become so used to being in a battle that when the war is over and we have survived, we do not know how to stop fighting so this fight becomes with ourselves and the battleground can become very bloody. It is important that we get through to ourselves that THE WAR IS OVER AND I HAVE WON.

Surrender is not a weakness, it is a strength. It is our ego mind that tells us it is so because it wants to keep us in a state of resistance. When we feel very resistant to something, it is important not to try and push through it but to take some time to remind ourselves that the battle is over and we are now surrendering to what is most beneficial to us. Wait until the resistance has gone and then get on with what is right for us to do. If we fight the resistance then we are perpetuating the battle. Once we have surrendered, we can hand the control over to our higher selves. This part of us is more than capable of helping us to manifest our heart's desire.

So let us look at some of the reasons for the resistance and see which of these may apply to us.

First, it is easy to stay small. We have a need to blend into the crowd, we don't like to be conspicuous or different. If we were with a large group of people all drowning and we were on dry land, we would probably jump in, in order to be accepted as one of the crowd. So here we all are thrashing about in a sea of lack and need, not daring to become visible by pulling ourselves out onto the shore of abundance. Peer pressure always tries to prevent us from standing out in a crowd.

Secondly, a status quo has probably been reached in our lives with our family, our relationships, our friends and our work. Therefore, there is an unwillingness to do anything to shake up this fine balance. If we suddenly became abundant and prosperous, could all these people in our lives cope with the changes, would they reject us or ostracise us? This is the fear. Once again, the reality is very different. Those people in our lives who genuinely want our highest good will always be there for us. Those who treat us like a doormat will either have to find another doormat or adjust to the changes in us, either way we benefit.

One of the things that people find particularly hard to acknowledge is a sense of their own power. It is often easier to be a victim than to admit that we are powerful beyond measure and create everything that happens to us in our lives. If we became abundant we would have to admit that we are powerful beings. (Yikes!!)

We will also look at the conflict between fearing failure and success. We fluctuate between the two. Sometimes putting our thoughts and actions into succeeding and sometimes into failing. The result once again is stalemate and we end up somewhere in between. The Universe cannot support us in our success or failure until it knows which option we have decided on.

So let us look at the options regarding this book and the plan it involves. What if we do it and it works, then we have to admit that we are powerful and that every area of our lives that are not working is actually down to us? We can no longer blame our parents, our partners, our education, our looks or any number of other things for what is wrong in our lives. (Scary?) What if we do it and it doesn't work? Well then all our worst fears are confirmed, we are useless, can't get anything right, will never amount to anything, why would anyone ever want to bother with us, we are just a waste of space etc.; the list would be endless. This is where the resistance plays an important part. If we give into the resistance and don't make the necessary changes of mind and shifts in order to make it work, then we will never have to face either of these options and we can live in a fantasy world that would always see us as a potential success but never actually putting it to the test. If this one rings true, don't worry, I think it is an almost universal truth.

The ego plays a large part in resistance. We will look at it in more detail later. The ego detests change, particularly change for the better. The more our lives are not working the happier our ego is because it means that it is in control. If we are abundant then we are working on the premise that the Universe is the source of all our worth and if we believe this then the ego has failed. Therefore, it will do everything in its power to stop this from happening. Fears are always fed to us from the ego and fears are always an illusion until we buy into them, then we give them energy and power. By thinking about them we file them into our belief systems and then end up creating the thing we feared. Then the ego tells us, "You see I was right to warn you about that one," and the whole process becomes reinforced. All the reasons we have already mentioned about why not to do this plan have been fed by the ego. Resistance and ego will always go hand in hand. Resistance comes up as a result of an unacknowledged truth. In this case I mainly believe that to be: "I am powerful enough to create my own reality".

If we experience our own resistance while doing the process, we need to acknowledge it and then focus on what we are wanting to achieve. Sometimes it seems easier to be stuck than to venture into uncharted territory no matter how great the rewards may be. We have a tendency to become addicted to our old patterns, feeling insecure at the thought of breaking out of them.

There is a time coming when abundance will be the order of the day. We have a choice as to whether we want to be a shepherd or a sheep. We can decide if we want to be one of the ones breaking new ground and then guiding others to follow us or will we wait until everyone else is doing it so that we can feel like one of the crowd. The choice is up to us.

EXERCISES

1) First of all check out how much resistance you have to being abundant.

2) Blank your mind and ask your unconscious on a scale of 1 - 100 how much resistance you have to an abundant life.

3) A number will come into your mind, don't try and second guess it or work it out beforehand. Our conscious mind does not know what beliefs and emotions are affecting us unconsciously. If a number does not pop into your mind immediately keep asking the question until it does, keeping the mind blank.

If you score 30% or under, this amount of resistance is at a level that is manageable, you are able to push through this wall of resistance.

If your score was between 30% and 70%, then resistance is playing a significant part in your life. This is too strong to ignore. Before you can begin to make shifts in your life the resistance must be dealt with.

If you scored over 70% then resistance is keeping you very stuck in your life. Resistance will stop you from doing anything that you want to do. It will feel like trying to swim through treacle. Even trying to do very mundane tasks will seem like an inner battle.

4) When faced with our resistance over any particular issue or action, it is really important to **RECOGNISE** it as resistance. When you know what you are dealing with you can do something about it.

a) Don't give yourself a hard time for having the resistance.

b) Check whether you really want to do or have what you are resistant to.

c) Notice what fears you have about this issue. Write them down and crud them (see Fear chapter).

d) Allow the resistance to subside before tackling the objective, by repeating:

I WILLINGLY LET GO MY RESISTANCE TO . . . . .

5) Write a declaration of surrender to yourself.

6) Affirm in it that the battles and the war are over and that from here on in all aspects of yourself will work in unity towards your purpose.

7) Sign it and burn it.

If your resistance is very strong there will be some ego issues which will be covered in the next chapter.

VISUALISATION

Relax into your chair, . . . let everything go. Take some deep breaths and with every out breath find yourself becoming more deeply relaxed . . . . Focus on a flame in the centre of your forehead . . . . Take that flame as a candle to guide you back through a corridor into your mind. Going deeper and deeper until you see a door at the end of the passage . . . . Open the door and step into a beautiful summer meadow . . . . Take in your surroundings, are there birds, insects and wild flowers? . . . . Start walking across the meadow towards a road . . . . When you reach the road you realise that this is the road to abundance . . . . You begin to go along this road and after a short distance you come up against a wall of resistance . . . . How big is it? . . . . What is it made of? . . . . How do you feel about it? . . . . Does it seem too overwhelming to you or is it easy to go through it? . . . . You can now start to dismantle your wall of resistance, use anything you need, dynamite or a bulldozer . . . . Clear every last bit of that wall away until your path is completely clear . . . . Ensure that the wall will not re-assemble itself . . . . When you are sure that your way is clear then move along your road to abundance knowing that there is no obstacle in your way. Begin to be aware of the abundant surroundings . . . . You feel yourself growing lighter, filled with joy and love and an excited expectancy . . . . All around you is everything you could ever need or desire, it is there for whenever you may want it . . . . Imprint this whole scene on your heart . . . . Know that it is always there inside you and is readily available . . . . Start back along your road towards your beautiful meadow . . . . Head across the meadow towards the door . . . . Open the door and pick up the candle to guide you along the corridor . . . . Focus on the flame in the centre of your forehead . . . . When you are ready come back into the room.

15

EGO

LETTING GO OF EGO IS THE KEY TO POWER

The ego is a very big subject to tackle, a whole book could be written about it and the influence and effect it has on our lives. I will endeavour to explain as simply as possible what is essentially an intangible aspect of us.

The ego is a master of disguise and may be hard to recognise in its many guises. It can be very subtle in its approach and is insidious. What is often understood by the ego is the macho image of someone who is very full of themself. We often associate egotism with the male of the species. However, this is only one small way in which the ego may manifest itself. The more common aspect of ego is low self-esteem. These people are always putting themselves down, feeling that they are not good enough at the things they do and thinking that they are undeserving of the things they want. This dynamic is very common in women and can often be reinforced by an abusive partner. This image is so far removed from our normal understanding of the ego that we may fail to recognise its origin.

The ego is inextricably linked with fear and it evolved hand in glove with it. The ego is constantly feeding us our fears. The ego fears death more than anything because it is linked with the mind and physical body. Consequently, when we die the ego dies with us.

The ego plays an important part in our development. Babies will associate themselves with their mothers until they are about eighteen months to two years old. After this they need to develop a sense of themselves as an individual. This is where the ego comes in and creates the terrible twos. It turns an angel of a baby into a monster of a child. Often this time becomes a battle between the egos of the parents and the child. However, this is also a very positive time as it allows the child to redefine their attitudes and ideas and this is also the time when children begin to learn to relate and interact with other children and adults.

The other thing that the ego fears apart from death is our higher or God self or soul. I will call it the Divine but it is all the same thing. This part of us is who we truly are, our personalities are just part of the package we have chosen for this lifetime. The Divine self cannot die, and it wants only good for us, it is perfect in every way, it loves unconditionally and if given the opportunity it will guide us and enable us to grow in enlightenment and consciousness. If we open up and allow ourselves to be guided by our Divine selves then the ego has absolutely no power over us at all. The ego will therefore do everything in its power to make sure that we don't open up spiritually and if we do, it will then often disguise itself as our Divine in order to fool us. There is a great deal of growth and learning to be obtained from our egos and since this is the whole purpose of our existence then it is important that we shift our perception and see the ego as our friend and not our enemy. I have often been amazed how many spiritual teachers and leaders are working from their egos and believing it to be their Divine selves.

As we have already seen in the resistance chapter, if we fight against our ego it will come to the forefront far more strongly and possibly destructively. Instead, it is necessary to use the positive qualities that the ego is capable of demonstrating and allowing them to work for you instead of against you. If we think our ego is only evil and destructive then these are the qualities that it will display to us. However, if we recognise the ego's intelligence, powers of observation, strength and abilities to create what it is giving its energy to, then we have a very powerful tool working in our favour. In a way, this process is like taming the monster;

it takes time and patience but the rewards are great.

The most positive thing that the ego has to give us is that it will show us **ALL** if our unhealed damage from the past. If we make the most of this, we can release and heal the things that are blocking our abundance by paying attention to the propaganda the ego feeds us.

One thing we need to create in our lives is a sense of balance. This involves balancing the ego and the Divine self. The ego is not totally negative, it has a great many gifts and abilities that can be very beneficial to us if we can access them. Equally, the Divine self, if not balanced by the ego can create problems and challenges in our lives. It would be very difficult to be grounded and work effectively on an Earth level. We are here to learn how to integrate all aspects of ourselves including the parts that may seem less than desirable.

The ego and Divine are part of the duality that we have on our three dimensional planet. This is often shown in cartoons where the character has an angel sitting on one shoulder and a devil on the other and both are putting their case forward. This is often more true in reality than we think. I myself have gone through phases where the battle between my ego and Divine has felt like world war two being re-inacted in the back of my head and often over the most trivial of matters. The end result would often be that I would be so exhausted by what had just taken place that I didn't have the energy to do what had emerged from the battle. The ego can be like a little devil or the serpent to Adam and Eve. It will try and tempt us away from our Divine pursuits, it will try and distract us from our endeavours. There is a story in the bible where Jesus goes into the wilderness for forty days and forty nights and he had a battle with the devil. This was not the devil but his ego. His ego wanted to tell him that he could give it all up and not have to go through the challenges of the last few months of his life. Obviously there were times when he was tempted to give in but eventually his Divine won out and he said "Get behind me Satan". They obviously did not know the term ego in biblical times but that is exactly what it was.

The ego has many weapons at its disposal. The most potent of these is fear. Ego uses fear where the Divine uses love. Fear is always an illusion! God created love but man creates fear. What we are afraid of does not exist until we create it with our powerful minds and it is the ego that puts it into our minds. If we are afraid of burglary, we often find that we are the ones who are burgled, when this happens instead of realising that we created that reality out of that fear, we allow ourselves to reinforce the fear. We think we were right to be fearful because it has happened and so we increase our fear which in turn increases the likelihood of it happening again. We hear stories of some people being burgled seven or eight times while their next door neighbours have never been burgled at all.

It is very important that when fears present themselves that we realise immediately what the source is and choose not to buy into them. The ego has no power at all unless we give it to it. This whole process is an unconscious one it has all taken place without us even being aware of it. We don't understand that it is we who are creating the adverse conditions in our lives and we then fall into the trap of believing that we are victims. If we bring what is unconscious out into our conscious mind then we can see where our ego has got a hold in our lives and then do something about it.

Another weapon that the ego uses is guilt. Guilt is always a choice we make. It is often a result of manipulation. This manipulation is either on the part of the ego of other people involved or else from our own ego. It will often occur after a decision arrived at through our Divine selves. The ego will then retaliate by trying to make that decision wrong to such an extent that we either change our minds or we have a thoroughly miserable time if we do it. Guilt will always try and tell us that we are selfish, mean, inconsiderate and put our own pleasures ahead of others. Religions thrive on using fear and guilt to bring people into line and most religions are run on ego. Guilt is a choice, in any given moment we can decide whether to feel it or not. Those people who seem to me to be almost addicted to guilt will usually be those with the least reason to feel it. We all know the scenario, these people give themselves selflessly to helping family and friends and then feel very guilty if they put themselves first for once! We often feel guilty about the resentment we feel when we do a lot for someone and don't get the appreciation it deserves or the return of energy we need in order not to become drained by that person. Because we feel guilty at feeling the resentment we sometimes try to make it up to the person by doing more for them!

How do we start recognising the ego? The ego uses comparisons all the time and it will either find us wanting or another person wanting. That person is much prettier, more clever, interesting, well off, funny or talented than us. It will know and hone in on our insecurities. Whatever we feel to be lacking in our lives, our egos will point out to us people who appear to have it and we will feel more and more devalued each time. In contrast it will also point out to us people who are not as pretty, clever, interesting, well off, funny or talented than us. It will tell us that at least we are better than that person, allowing us to feel superficially superior. The reason we need to have this is because we actually feel very bad about ourselves and we need to offload some of this onto someone else.

Tyranny is always a result of the ego and feeling

substandard. A tyrant will always look for a victim. The victim is usually someone who appears to be weak or vulnerable, the tyrant is too much of a coward to pick on someone who is secure in themselves. The ego will also judge people all the time, it needs to find people wrong, it is unable to accept people and situations just as they are. This is the province of the Divine self which will see everybody as a perfect child of light. It may observe that each soul has made some choices which seem to obscure this Divine Light from others in which case they need love, support and compassion, not condemnation. The Divine encourages us to learn and grow from people and situations and when we have done that we are able to move on.

Jealousy and envy is another area that allows the ego to run amok. Jealousy is born out of the ego's need for comparisons and it is a very corrosive emotion. It destroys relationships, friendships and creates disharmony in the world. The ego will fuel the jealousy with more comparisons and judgements. The positive outcome from this to the ego is that we then become consumed by the jealous thoughts. We are certainly not listening to anything that our Divine self is trying to get through to us. This results in a victory for the ego.

So let us look now at how the ego is blocking abundance in our lives. Let me say at this point that for some people, far from blocking their wealth, the ego created it. The need to prove ourselves better than everyone else, out of a feeling of inferiority, comes straight from the ego. We have all seen that scenario of working class boy makes good. However, for these people whatever they have doesn't seem to be enough because money doesn't banish those feelings of inferiority, so the ego has a field day. Anyone reading this book probably doesn't come into that category, so we will not dwell on that aspect.

As I have already stated, the ego is most threatened by

our Divine selves and it is through our Divine that abundance is going to come, so this is the area in which it targets. The ego will tell us that money is evil and therefore we, as spiritual beings, should have nothing to do with it. It will tell us that we should be totally selfless, give everything away to others and allow ourselves to suffer and struggle. It will make us guilty for having or wanting money. In this instance the ego is very much in disguise because most people would think that these thoughts are coming from the Divine. We really need to understand that the Universe wants us to be abundant and any thoughts or beliefs to the contrary do not come from our Divine.

The ego will always make judgements about people who do have money: it will make them wicked, vain, exploitative and wrong. I remember one day sitting in an outdoor cafe near Covent Garden. There was a Rolls Royce parked in a meter nearby. The meter had expired and a tow-away van was lifting the car onto it, a crowd had gathered and began to clap and a man commented to my friend and me, "It makes you feel good doesn't it". I was quite shocked at this. Nobody knew who this person was, the one thing they knew about him or her was that they were wealthy and they were prepared to dislike them on that basis alone. This is the ego at work.

The ego is also the source of our fears about money. It will feed us fears about having money and also fears about not having money. We will look at fears in more detail. The effect of these fears is that they all but paralyse us. We don't dare have money but we fear not having it.

The ego hates change so when we reach various points in our lives when change is on the cards, the ego will come to the forefront. It is quite positive to notice that when the ego is most active is when it is under threat and this is usually when we are acting upon guidance from our Divine, so it is very important that we recognise it for what it is and don't allow it to destroy what is good and joyful in our lives.

The ego will try to make us guilty when we do have some money; it might remind us how immoral it is for us to have abundance when there are people starving in third world countries or it will question what we choose to spend it on. While doing this plan someone in one of my groups came into a windfall of £900. I noticed that she didn't seem to be enjoying this and she didn't even mention it in the group. When I brought it up we found that her ego was having a field day. It told her that because she had not worked hard for this money it was not something she deserved to enjoy. She feared spending it because then it would be gone and she would feel she had wasted it. She also felt that she had manipulated it, and that if she spent it on herself and not on her family she was being selfish and greedy. The result of this is that not only does she not feel any joy at this windfall but she actually felt bad about it. Out of this comes the belief that money does not make us happy, it makes us unhappy. A victory for the ego. It is not that money or abundance makes us happy or unhappy, it is merely a question of whether we choose to be happy and enjoy it. It doesn't matter whether this is a little or a lot, what does matter is whether we experience any sense of limitation due to lack of money.

There are some exercises to follow dealing with the ego. Trying to ignore the ego and pretend it doesn't exist does not work because it then becomes more devious and possibly more destructive. The challenge we face is learning to understand the ego, recognise when it is at work and not giving energy to its machinations. By doing this we can master it and learn to integrate the ego into our lives.

EXERCISES

1) The first step in dealing with the ego is recognising it and seeing how it is affecting your life.

2) Take some time each day, a minimum of 5 minutes, monitoring your thoughts.

3) The ego will reveal itself in any of the following ways:

a)   It will present you with a judgement or criticism about yourself or others.

b)   It will inject fears, some rational, some irrational.

c)   It will want to apportion blame, sometimes onto others, sometimes onto yourself, always making someone wrong.

d)   It will try to block any move you make to improve yourself or your life. It wants to keep you stuck. Usually this is done by giving you reasons why you don't need it. Resistance!

4) When you have identified a negative ego thought you can neutralise it by saying CANCEL.

5) If it feels like the ego is dominating, then visualise a balloon and then burst it with a pin. See the ineffective piece of rubber that results.

6) The ego, like a child, does not like to be ignored, if you do ignore it, it will only shout louder. When your ego is trying to impress its opinion on you, acknowledge the source and then thank it for its contribution and let it go.

7) When you notice a negative feeling or belief being fed to you by the ego. Recognise that this is an illusion that has not been healed from the past.

8) Find out why your ego self does not want you to have an abundant life.

VISUALISATION

Relax into your chair . . . . Take some deep breaths and with every outbreath you find you become more deeply relaxed . . . . Focus on a flame in the centre of your forehead . . . . Take that flame as a candle to guide you down a long corridor into your subconscious mind . . . . At the end of this corridor there is a door . . . . Open this door into a beautiful summer meadow . . . . Take in the flowers and butterflies and the sky and the sun . . . . At the other side of the meadow you can see a rock escarpment filled with dark caves. The height of the escarpment blocks the sun from entering the caves. . . . From where you are standing you can see that there is one cave that is larger than the others . . . . Walk towards that cave now . . . . Within this cave dwells your ego . . . . When you get near the cave you can see that it is so dark that you cannot see a thing . . . . Note how you feel about going inside and confronting your ego . . . . Taking a candle or torch with you, go inside the cave . . . . What form do you think your ego is taking? . . . . It could be like a person or an animal or something more abstract . . . . Observe what you can of it with the light source available . . . . How does it feel about seeing you face to face? . . . . Begin a dialogue with your ego, listen to its grievances and fears . . . . Do not become defensive or aggressive. Just allow it to have its say . . . . Watch its response . . . . Then guide your ego out of the cave and into the sunlight, see a particularly strong shaft of light surround you and your ego and watch as a transformation takes place . . . . What form does your ego take now? . . . . Tell your ego that you love it and give it a hug . . . . Explain to it that from here on in you will be working in harmony together, and that the ego will no longer be trying to fight for control and domination . . . . and then watch as your ego merges with you . . . . Integrating totally into your being . . . . Before you go make sure that the cave is now filled in . . . . Then return across the meadow to your door . . . . Open the door and pick up the candle to guide you back down the corridor . . . . Then focus on the flame in the centre of your forehead . . . . When you are ready bring your attention back into the room.

You may need to repeat this visualisation a few times.

MENTAL BELIEFS

SOWING POSITIVE SEEDS IS THE KEY TO AN ABUNDANT HARVEST

The first part of this plan deals with mental beliefs in our lives. We probably have heard it said many times that what we think and believe creates our reality. This means that we have to begin to take responsibility for what happens to us. In order to make changes in our lives we have to change our minds. The problem we face here is that probably up to 90% of our beliefs are unconscious, so how do we change what we don't even know we have? Many people do affirmations in order to reprogram the unconscious mind. My feeling about this is that affirmations will only work long term if we first remove the firmly entrenched beliefs that are creating the destructive patterning. For me, The unconscious mind is like a field and every negative belief is like a weed which has seeded itself in the field; every time we have a thought that reinforces that belief it is like feeding and watering that weed. When we say an affirmation, which is like a positive seed planted, the weed which is strong and well rooted will overpower that little seed and choke it so that it does not come to fruition. In order for this process to work we must first weed out the negative beliefs before planting the positive seeds and keeping them fed and watered with positive thoughts.

So how do we start to weed out these negative beliefs? First of all, it is important to recognise that this is an ongoing process and we need the discipline to keep doing it. It is no good pulling out two weeds and expecting the field to yield an abundant harvest. The first stage is to begin to know what the beliefs are. Some will be conscious beliefs so we can identify these first. Our conscious beliefs and those that subconsciously control our lives are very different. It is important that we don't get fooled into thinking that what we know we believe to be the only influence. Our conscious mind is such a small percentage of our whole mind. Let me say at this stage that we also have plenty of positive beliefs that are working well for us. The next stage is uncovering the unconscious beliefs. Some of these we will have inherited from our parents. Some come from society, some from any religious teaching. Some we will have picked up from television and the media, others will be from our own observations of what is going on around us, particularly in childhood. Most of these unconscious beliefs will have been picked up in childhood. The unconscious mind is like a computer being programmed all the time. As children we are like sponges and we are also great observers of life. However, our experience does not always allow us to put a correct interpretation onto a certain situation and therefore we may program into our computer minds a totally false belief or illusion. Many of our beliefs may be totally conflicting; we may believe money is good and that money is bad. One parent may believe that money is to be spent while the other believes that money is to be saved, so we inherit both those beliefs and what this might result in is an inner conflict. Every time we spend money we are wrong, and every time we save it we are wrong.

When we are not aware of our unconscious beliefs, we have to view the process in reverse. We can find out our beliefs by looking at the circumstances that our beliefs have manifested. We only need to look at our lives. Look for the clues, work with the mirror of life and everything we need to know is there.

Obviously just identifying our beliefs is not enough to actually remove them, it is only the first stage. With my clients I use a process I call crudding. This is not just for mental beliefs but for anything I want to remove from the spiritual, mental, emotional and physical bodies.

EXERCISES

1) For this process you need a metal bucket in which to burn paper. Having identified the belief system you then crud it as follows: Write on a piece of paper.

   I RELEASE the belief that . . . . .

   3 times. Then underneath put:-

   ## I REMOVE THIS BELIEF FROM MY UNCONSCIOUS MIND ONCE AND FOR ALL.

2) This is then burnt in the metal bucket outside. Observe how well and quickly the paper burns. If it is very slow or you have to relight it again it shows that there is resistance to letting it go and therefore it may need to be done two or three times. I have seen two people crudding on similar paper with the same weather conditions where one piece of paper is consumed immediately while the other person may have to relight it five or six times.

3) Once the belief system has been crudded, affirm.

   ## I DESERVE ABUNDANCE IN ALL AREAS OF MY LIFE.

4) Other aspects that I use crudding for are: Releasing fears, dealing with negative situations, i.e. instead of going over and over in your mind when something unpleasant happens you write it down, including your emotional response to the situation, and then burn it, this speeds up the letting go process. I also advise people to clear old emotions and situation by writing a letter to the person involved and then burning it, even if that person is now dead. Burning is a very powerful releasing tool and can have many other uses as well. We can also use burning as a way of expanding good things in our life, such as lists of what we are grateful for and writing out when a good thing happens.

5) What are your conscious beliefs about money? Many of these will be positive so write them out and keep them.

6) CRUD the negative beliefs using the technique above.

WOMEN AND MONEY

The issues facing women and money are totally different from those of men, so we are going to look at them separately. Most books written about prosperity are written by men and they fail to address the subject from a female perspective.

For thousands and thousands of years now women have not been allowed to have their own money or a say in how to spend it. This has only begun to change in the latter part of the twentieth century. The catalyst for this transformation was the second world war, where due to a lack of manpower, women were put into previously men only jobs. This gave them a sense of confidence, independence and self-worth, qualities they were unwilling to give up when the men came back from war. This gave way to the female revolution which is still very much in progress. As I have said, the new order is going to be ushered in by the female principle. This can be seen clearly when attending any personal or spiritual development group. Seventy to eighty percent of those there will be women. The feminism that started in the sixties tried to gain equality with men by trying to become more like men. All this created was more male energy. This happened again in the eighties when suddenly women were being given high powered jobs, positions in authority over men, they felt that in order to be accepted in this male world they had to suppress their femininity in order to succeed. Even sex became a power issue.

The fact is that a woman's power lies in her female qualities, intuition, nurturing, receiving, beauty, harmony and love and it is through these qualities that man's salvation lies.

Money and abundance seems to be one of the biggest stumbling blocks for women. Those who are aware and are using those female qualities in their life are finding that there is very little financial remuneration resulting. Many find themselves stuck in marriages they can't afford to get out of, or else doing a tedious job that does not allow them to feel spiritually or creatively fulfilled. Jobs that do allow for the female principle are notoriously badly paid. Nurses and teachers are expected to do their jobs because they have a vocation not because they want to earn a decent living.

It is interesting to notice that within a relationship money and power are inextricably linked. I have noticed in many instances where the female is the dominant partner, the man will hand over his pay packet, the woman would then assume the responsibility of paying all the bills and household expenses and he would be given beer money. In contrast I had one client who was not given a single penny by her husband. She was not deprived but she had to ask him for everything she wanted and if he didn't approve then she couldn't get it. Her friends would even have to subsidise her to come and see me. At a later session she was excited because she had started a part time job. I said how pleased I was that she would have some money of her own to spend but she revealed that nothing had changed. Her wages were paid straight into a joint account that she was not allowed to touch and she still had to ask for whatever she needed. Her husband had told her that she was stupid with money and couldn't be trusted to spend it wisely. This particular lady's self worth and confidence were at rock bottom and she totally believed her husband's estimation of herself.

There are still other relationships where the power base is far more balanced. In these relationships there is often a joint account into which either partner can dip at will or else the woman earns a high enough salary in her own right not to need any subsidy from her partner.

The meteoric rise of women that has occurred in the last few decades has shaken many men who feel emasculated by it. Out of this fear of losing the male dominance in society, a new tyranny has been born. This tyranny is expecting women to fit into an unrealistic standard of physical perfection and in not attaining it they become devalued as a person. There are very few women who have not succumbed to this pressure, even those who vociferously claim they haven't will at some level measure their self esteem on physical lines. Those who do attain the standard are then desperate to hang onto it as ageing begins to take its toll. Men do not have this pressure put on them and are chiefly behind the myth of female perfection. One way in which I have noticed that this has affected the question of abundance adversely is over the question of food. In the western world we have a huge variety and amount of food available to us in the supermarkets and yet for most women this conjures feelings of temptation, guilt and self-disgust. Here is a situation where abundance which should be positive has taken on such negative connotations.

That this is a female issue is born out by a study which took five couples where the woman usually did the food shopping. They got both partners to do a weekly shop for their family of four. In every case the men spent 50-100% more than the woman but bought scarcely enough to cover one family meal. The men had bought mainly alcohol, cakes, biscuits, snacks, sweets and red meat. If a woman had bought the same ingredients there would have been feelings of guilt and lacking in self-discipline.

In order for women to move abundantly in the world we have got to work through thousands of years of conditioning and beliefs.

Women were never expected to have or manage any money. They would go from being taken care of by their father to having a husband assuming the same responsibilities. Even though times have changed the basic underlying belief has not. We are all brought up with fairy-tales. The theme of most of these stories are similar, a beautiful young girl comes through adversity, meets Prince Charming and lives happily ever after. To a greater or lesser degree we have all bought into this myth. There is a secret hope that our knight in shining armour will sweep us off our feet and take care of us in every way until death do us part. The fairy-tale wedding reinforces the whole myth for this is where the father formally hands over his daughter to the husband. It is soon after the wedding that disillusion sets in and the myth begins to dissolve. Far from finding that the man is going to take care of her from here on in, the reality is that she will be taking care of him, doing a job, running a home, doing his washing, ironing, cooking, cleaning and looking after children when they come along. At this point instead of seeing the fairy-tale for what it is we convince ourselves that it was just that this was a rat masquerading as Prince Charming and that the real one is still out there. Seventy percent of divorces are initiated by women and I think this statistic would be much higher if some women believed that they could manage financially on their own.

Feminism has also given us the myth of "Having It All", which says that a woman should be able to have a high powered, well paid job, a couple of children, a big house and a husband. It fails to point out that there are not enough hours in the day to do justice to all of them, the result of this is a great deal of stress and guilt.

It is important that we weed out our own and society's beliefs concerning women and money as these beliefs belong to a time in the past that does not exist anymore. We can envisage then the part women have to play during and after this transitional phase and create new belief systems to fit those new roles.

The time is close whereby women can be whole and consequently attract partners who are also whole and then we can move forward and work with them in harmony if we so choose.

EXERCISES

1) It is important to do this process whether you are male or female.
2) What beliefs do you have about women and money?
3) Do not worry if some of these are contradictory.

4) See notes at the back of the book for some common beliefs that may apply to you.

5) Remove as many of the negative beliefs as possible by CRUDDING THEM: Write on paper.

I RELEASE the belief that . . . .

Three times. Then underneath put:-

I REMOVE THIS FROM MY UNCONSCIOUS MIND ONCE AND FOR ALL.

Burn.

6) You may need to do this several times if the belief is particularly entrenched.

7) Keep and notice any beliefs that serve you.

MEN AND MONEY

This is a subject that I am obviously less qualified to deal with. The stresses men are facing are very different than those confronting women. Man's traditional role as the provider, the hunter gatherer, has begun to be challenged by changes in society. High unemployment and redundancies right across the board have meant that in many households the woman is the main earner.

Also, due to the breakdown of marriages a man may be expected to provide for two or even three families on a salary that can hardly maintain one. The large number of suicides since the start of the Child Support Agency attests to this. This must seem to be an insoluble problem for many men and the amount of fear, anger and resentment it creates breaks down relationships.

A man's self esteem is very much tied in with his ability to provide for himself and his family. In the western industrialised world there has been a huge restructuring in the industries. Areas which were dedicated to ship building or mining in various areas of Britain are now virtually without means of employment. A large proportion of men are unemployed without any hope of a job. The main growth area for employment is in computers and this usually employs the young who feel comfortable with this new technology. In so many homes the wife is the sole provider, doing jobs that do not pay well and often having to do two or three jobs just to make ends meet. Nothing in history has prepared men for dealing with this situation and the cost to the human condition is very pricey. For so many of these people it must seem like there is no way out. Another strata of men who are suffering are white collar workers in their late forties and fifties. Many of these have been working in good, well paid jobs and due to redundancy have found themselves put out to grass in their prime. Many companies have a policy not to recruit new staff over a certain age. The legacy to the people involved is devastating. Many have to accept the fact that they may never work again with perhaps forty years of life stretching in front of them. It is essential that society stops forcing men to identify themselves so completely with what they do and not with who they are.

Statistics show that the size of a man's wallet has much to do with his attractiveness to women. She is often prepared to overlook physical shortcomings if his ability to wine and dine is obvious. The expectation many women have to be taken care of financially and the heavy burden this puts on a man can seem like a yoke around his neck. Many men will work their whole lives in jobs they dislike just to fulfil this obligation, never discovering their true gifts and abilities.

Jesus if he appeared today, far from being hailed as the Messiah, would probably be vilified and condemned as a New Age Traveller. He would have looked scruffy and hippyish with long hair. His words would have been dismissed as idealistic clap trap and his whole manner would probably convince people that he was on drugs. The chances are that his message would have gone unheard apart from a few followers.

In many ways men have far more barriers to prosperity and abundance than women do. Women are starting with a clean sheet on which to create. Whereas men have to dismantle thousands of years of conditioning before they can bring in the new abundance. I have one very close friend who always says that the meaning of life is to pay his bills. He is on a very good salary that for most people would provide a comfortable standard of living. However, due to some unfortunate house deals and negative equity, he is living in rented accommodation paying high interest on the debt and at the end of each month he only manages to pay his bills. No extras at all.

I have another friend whose attitude is totally different. He believes that life is to be enjoyed. His salary is about a third of that of my other friend. He was renting a tiny flat in a huge double fronted house when the landlord informed him that he was selling the whole house and did he want to buy it. He quoted a give away price and even gave him a mortgage. He then sold it for nearly three times the original price. He now has a beautiful four bedroom house and enough money in the bank to do whatever he wants.

In each of these cases the Universe is showing each of these men exactly what their beliefs and expectations about money are. An observer might just say that one had had bad luck and the other good but every single thing we believe about money is manifesting in our lives right now, some may be good, some may be bad. If we want to change our prosperity then we have to change the core beliefs that have created our reality. The Universe can only create the miracles we want when we resonate with that belief.

We are in the middle of dismantling the old way of working and this is why men seem to be suffering more than women. Men feel like they are losing control over their lives and their ability to make money whereas women appear to be gaining more control than ever before. It is because most men do not see that in order to have what is better we must first get rid of what does not work. Instead they feel like they are being pulled into an abyss without safety ropes. This is causing a great deal of fear and this fear will often bring out more aggression.

The lot of man is about to be transformed and improved out of all recognition. If we can embrace this without fear and without needing to know exactly how it will look then the road ahead will be exciting and filled with wonder.

EXERCISES

1) What are your beliefs about Men and Money.

2) CRUD the negative ones.

3) This needs to be done by males and females.

See notes at the back of the book for some common beliefs poeple have.

MOTHER AND FATHER'S BELIEFS

It is easy to feel overwhelmed by the sheer volume of mental beliefs we have. For this reason it is easier to tackle them if we split them up into categories. We will start with our parents' beliefs, these are the first examples we have of understanding how money works. When we were first given pocket money were we encouraged to spend it or save it. Could we choose what we spent it on or did we have to have their approval?

Our parents will have many and varying beliefs about money because they in turn are the products of their parents. They will also be affected if they or their parents lived through the deprivations of the second world war. When we start to look at our parents' money beliefs we can see how conflicting many of them are, it is no wonder money causes such rifts within a relationship. My own mother absolutely abhors waste, she will eat bad fruit rather than throw it away and she even washes cling film and rinses it to save a few pennies. In contrast she will spend vast sums on quality clothes and furnishings.

Even when we consciously reject some of our parents beliefs they will still be affecting us on an unconscious level so it is important to be aware of them even if we don't think we have them.

Some of our parents' money beliefs will work positively for us without our even being aware of it. To some extent we have an expectation that our adult incomes will be similar to that of our parents. We tend to choose jobs or marry men that will put us into the same financial bracket. For my last two years at school I went to a boys' public school in the middle of the stockbroker belt. I went to an old boys' day about seven years after leaving school, most of the boys had either followed their fathers into lucrative jobs in the city or were doctors or lawyers. No doubt these jobs were as a result of some mental programming started in childhood.

EXERCISES

1) Discover as many of your parents' beliefs about money as you can. Make two lists, one with beliefs that are negative or do not fit in with your life philosophy. The other list is beliefs of your parents that are positive that fit in with what you want from life.

2) Look at what your parent's expectations of you were.

3) Have you lived up to them?

4) If so, do you feel that you are living your life as you would want it.

5) If not, do you feel guilty or a failure?

6) Notice if you are a rebel and have completely rejected your parents values. Be careful that you do not throw the baby out with the bath water. Some of their beliefs will have a positive affect on you.

7) CRUD the negative beliefs.

MASS BELIEFS BLOCKING PROSPERITY

We all have hundreds of beliefs about prosperity and abundance that create our own personal money reality. However, there are a few beliefs that most people share that then create a mass consciousness that serves to reinforce our own negative beliefs. The first of these is the scarcity principle. This is a belief in lack, that there is not enough to go round. That when the prosperity pie gets sliced up, some people will be given too much, others just enough to survive on while others will get nothing at all. Even if this pie was divided fairly among all humanity, each share would be hardly enough to survive on. We are living in the most populated time in history and that population is only going to grow so in effect our share can only get smaller. We have already taken most of the resources the Earth has to offer. Given these facts, the future for humanity certainly looks bleak. The gap between the haves and have nots is getting wider. For the haves it seems that everyone is trying to get their prosperity off them by fair means or foul. While the have nots are becoming increasingly frustrated and resentful at their lot. The mistake we have made in buying into this belief is that abundance and prosperity come from a finite source, that there is no more. Whereas the reality is that abundance comes from an infinite source, it is totally unlimited. Because we don't believe this we block this energy from manifesting. We see our planet as being the be all and end all of all existence. It is actually such a tiny part of the whole cosmos and a very backward part at that. The Earth is like a little colony of ants who believe that they are the master race and that the boundaries of their group are all that exists and that when all the food from within this area is gone then that is it. That is not their reality anymore than it is ours.

Another major and almost universal belief is often created in childhood. We are either told or are given the impression that we are not clever enough, pretty enough, good enough, funny enough, sporty enough, confident enough, artistic enough, etc., the list goes on. Whichever of these beliefs we have taken on board, the result is the thought that we are not enough. Most people will have this belief to a greater or lesser degree. Out of this belief we then unconsciously rationalise that because we are not enough we do not deserve to have things in life that will make us feel good. This doesn't just affect prosperity but all aspects of life. Love and relationships, career, fulfilment, creativity and so on. As I have said this process is usually an unconscious one but I have noticed in my groups that even when we become conscious of it and are given a choice as to whether to go down a path which will bring fear and struggle or to go down one that brings joy, love and fulfilment, most people end up choosing the former. Others witnessing this situation are often amazed and yet when they find themselves in a similar situation, their response is often the same. The ego has a great deal to do with this as it will always try to convince us that we are not enough. Contrary to this our Divine self knows that we are perfect children of the Universe and to deny ourselves and our perfection is to deny the highest part of ourselves. Our egos will usually come back with "You special! Who do you think you are? Don't make me laugh."

We have a choice as to whether we buy into our egos or our Divines estimation of ourselves. Note that when we take on board our Divine's viewpoint we are not becoming big headed with it because we can also see that every other person on the planet is also a perfect child of the Universe. There are no evil people, only people who have chosen fear, which hides their shining lights from others.

It is very important that we remove the beliefs in scarcity, not being enough and not deserving our highest good from the unconscious mind. Each of these beliefs will have been reinforced hundreds of times, when we are rejected by others, don't get a job, are ridiculed etc. so the following process is designed to remove the initial beliefs and all the reinforcing thoughts and beliefs.

EXERCISES

1) Write a list of ways in which you believe or have been told that you are not enough. e.g. I am not clever enough, I am not attractive enough, etc.

2) Beside each one, check out on a scale of 1 - 10 how much you believe this to be true?

3) CRUD these beliefs. These may be so entrenched that you may need to do this more than once.

4) Release your belief in scarcity by crudding it:

I RELEASE THE BELIEF THAT THERE IS A SCARCITY OF MONEY AND RESOURCES ON EARTH.

Three times.

VISUALISATION

Sit comfortably and close your eyes and relax. Take some deep breaths and just let everything go. You are going to go on a journey to the control room of your unconscious mind. See yourself as you are in the chair and then see yourself getting smaller and smaller, shrinking all the time, ... getting smaller still . . . . When you are about the size of a finger nail, you are going to travel inside your body, so put tiny you onto your own tongue and begin to journey up from the back of the throat, . . . Through the nasal cavities . . . . until you reach a door . . . . This is the door to your unconscious mind . . . . Open the door and enter into the computer control room of your unconscious. . . . There is a large computer consul straight ahead of you . . . . With a chair in front of it . . . . Sit down on that chair and switch on the computer . . . . The keyboard is in front of you and the screen lights up . . . . You are going to bring onto the screen all the beliefs and thoughts you have had about deserving prosperity, beliefs in scarcity and being not good enough . . . Type onto the computer the following words:

NEGATIVE BELIEFS AND THOUGHTS ABOUT NOT DESERVING PROSPERITY.

When this is typed onto the screen press the enter key. . . . and then search key . . . . You will see all these beliefs appear on the screen, there may be hundreds of these beliefs . . . . Press the delete button and watch as all these disappear from the computer and from your unconscious mind once and for all . . . . You do not need to know exactly what the beliefs are, just watch them disappear from the screen . . . . Keep your finger on the delete button until the screen is clear . . . .

Now you are going to type in a new belief system to replace the old negative beliefs . . . . So type onto the screen:

I DESERVE ABUNDANCE AND PROSPERITY . . . .

Press the enter key and watch as this new belief instantly fills the screen filling all the space in the computer previously taken up with the old beliefs.

Now you are going to repeat the process by typing onto the screen:

NEGATIVE BELIEFS AND THOUGHTS ABOUT SCARCITY AND LACK.

Then press the enter key . . . . then press the search key. . . . See all your beliefs appear on the screen then press and keep pressing the delete key until all the words on the screen have disappeared . . . . Then type in the new belief:

I HAVE GREAT ABUNDANCE AVAILABLE TO ME AT ALL TIMES.

Press the enter key and see the screen filling up with this new belief replacing the space taken up by the old.

Now repeat the process again.

Type onto the screen:

NEGATIVE BELIEFS AND THOUGHTS THAT I AM NOT GOOD ENOUGH.

Press the enter key then press search key. See the screen fill up and press the delete button. See the screen clear . . . . type in the new belief:

I AM ENOUGH. I AM THAT I AM.

Press the enter key . . . See the space being filled with the new beliefs.

When this is done switch off the computer knowing that you can return at any time to reprogram old beliefs . . . . Come out of the computer room and return down through the sinus cavities . . . Down to the back of the throat and onto your tongue . . . . Return tiny you onto the chair and see yourself growing bigger and bigger . . . . Bigger and bigger until you reach your normal size . . . . Then when you are ready return your attention back into the room.

Repeat this visualisation until no beliefs appear on the screen when called up.

MONEY AND SPIRITUALITY

For many people who have chosen a spiritual path abundance seems to be a particular problem. This is partly due to a belief, sometimes unconscious and sometimes conscious, that to be spiritual means denouncing the material world. At the same time we have to live in the material world, we need a roof over our heads, food, clothing, transportation and so on. So we have a conflict here. Very often spiritual people find themselves in financial difficulties and the worry and fears that are created out of this end up blocking the very thing that they most want to achieve.

We are given the message that our spirit and money are incompatible. The bible tells us that it is easier for a camel to go through the eye of a needle than for a rich man to get to Heaven. Monks and nuns take vows of poverty and yet the religions they represent are some of the richest institutions in the world. There seems to me to be a degree of hypocrisy in this. A friend of mine had a grandmother who lived in Ireland. She had a house with no heating and no hot water. While his sister was visiting she found an envelope with over eight hundred pounds in cash. When she asked her grandmother about it she was told that it was for the priest when he called. This lady believed that she was buying a place in Heaven by giving to the church out of her meagre pension. This money either went to keeping the Priest in the standard he was accustomed to or else if it was given to a charity case, it was probably not to anyone more deserving than she was.

This point in history is about the uniting of our inner selves and the world "out there". In order for the Earth and its people to heal themselves the spiritual world and material world need to embrace each other.

There are aspects of abundance that are incompatible with our spirituality. One of these is greed, another is the worship of money. Another is when money is used as a power tool to exert fear and undue influence over other people. In every case money is not the cause, it is the weapon used.

For those who have given up jobs that had brought in a decent income in favour of doing work which has more of a spiritual bent, some are finding it difficult to make a living

45

because there is a prejudice which makes it wrong to take money for gifts that are so called "God given", like healing and spiritual counselling. However, where energy is used, in order for that person not to become drained, an exchange of energy must take place. It need not necessarily be money and it does need to be agreed upon in advance. This prejudice seems to reinforce the belief that if we choose a spiritual path we give up any thoughts of abundance and prosperity. This is a difficult belief for many people to shake off.

We also see some sense of nobility in suffering when done for a spiritual cause. All those people in history who suffered religious persecution or gave up everything for their faith are often the examples that we are expected to follow in order to come up to scratch. The natural state that the Universe intended for us is to be abundant. There are no extra brownie points for needless self imposed suffering or sacrifice. This is another area that the ego has a field day with. The ego will always compare us with others and usually find us wanting. It will tell us that if we are such a spiritual person then we shouldn't need money, we should welcome pain and suffering because we are showing the Universe how much you are willing to put up with, that poverty and service go hand in hand. The pay off for the ego in this is that a great deal of our energy is then used up in basic issues of survival, coping with the pain and deprivation and there is very little left to put into what is really the Universe's ministry for us here on Earth.

For ourselves we often find a level that we judge acceptable to have money. This is usually somewhere from just above the survival level to somewhere well below the abundance level. While we stay within these boundaries we can feel we are not compromising our spiritual status by succumbing to the temptation of the material world.

46

However, these boundaries create limitation which prevents us from using the very energy that we are wanting to bring in with our spiritual practices, because incorporated in that energy is abundance.

EXERCISES

1) What beliefs do you have about money and spirituality being incompatible?
2) Make a list and CRUD them.
3) See notes at the back for possible beliefs you may have missed.

FOUR BODIES

We are made up of four bodies. The spiritual body, the mental body, the emotional body and the physical body. It is important that we deal with a person as a whole and therefore we need to address all four of these bodies. Very often when we are trying to make changes in any area of our lives, we only focus on one or possibly two of these bodies and fail to deal with the others. Most therapies will only deal with one body.

In looking at abundance we need to observe how we may have created blocks in each of these bodies because it is only when all the blocks have cleared that there is a complete free flow of energy which is what creates total and absolute abundance in our lives.

The blocks that are created on a spiritual level may be from a past life or two. Perhaps we have abused the use of money in a lifetime or had too many lifetimes where we have been poor. Whatever the reason, maybe we just have to acknowledge and clear it. We no longer have to live out our karma but we do have to let it go. So don't fall into the trap of thinking that because we have chosen to be born into a life of poverty or hardship that has to be our lot for the rest of this life. Karma is just there to be cleared. Another block that can occur on a spiritual level is the failure to see the Universe as the source of all our abundance. This occurs when we give into the ego's propaganda that money and spirituality are completely incompatible.

The mental body probably provides most blocks that stand in the way of abundance. These are all the belief systems that we have taken on from society, our families and our own personal experiences. Since we are not living in an abundance conscious world, most of these beliefs will be negative. The ego also works through the mental body and the ego is the biggest single block we have to abundance. The mind is the source of manifestation and if we are not manifesting what we want in our lives then we need to look for the blocks in the mental body.

The main blockage that occurs on the emotional body is fear and this can be crippling if it is allowed to take a hold. Other emotions that can have an adverse effect are guilt, anger, resentment and jealousy. The emotional and mental bodies can work quite closely together with the ego triggering thoughts that in turn feed these emotions I have just mentioned.

The physical body is where everything manifests. It is where we see the results of the blockages on the other bodies. We often make the mistake of thinking that because imbalances make themselves known on the physical that this is where they need to be treated. This completely ignores the real source of the problem. It is very often the physical body that shows us what needs to be healed if we start to read the clues that it is giving us.

EMOTIONAL BODY

Fear

LIGHT IS THE KEY TO BANISHING FEAR

Like the ego, fear played an important part in the survival of early man. If we feared wild animals, the elements and starvation then we would take active steps to protect ourselves against them. However, once fear got a hold we then created things to fear. Fear is always an illusion until we create the very thing we are afraid of. Nowadays, because of television, newspapers and the ease of world travel we are able to see first hand the atrocities that go on all over the world and because of this we are much more fearful and we create more negative situations. It then becomes a vicious circle. Most of the things we fear now, a hundred years ago either did not exist or we would have been blissfully unaware of them. Cars and planes and many aspects of new technology create a great deal of fear in people.

Fears affect abundance in two main ways. Fears about not having it and fears about having it. In the western world now starvation has virtually been irradicated due to welfare benefits. Lack of a video or music system now makes us on the breadline these days. However, for many who have mortgages and young families and a car to run, fears about not being able to support and maintain these are very real. Redundancy or threat of it has created a great deal of fear, particularly for many men whose self-esteem is tied up in their ability to provide. For women the fear of not being able to maintain their standard of living may keep them stuck in a marriage that has long since broken down.

The fears about having money and abundance can be even greater. Fear of the responsibility, fear of losing friends, fear of inciting jealousy in others. Fear of being conned or taken for a ride. Fear of finding that it doesn't bring happiness. Fear of it putting off genuine people coming into our lives and attracting those who are only out for what they can get. All these and more play a large part in blocking any abundance coming, unless they are dealt with. We are always finding real life situations that back up these fears and so reinforce them.

It is important that we first acknowledge that fears are an illusion until our subconscious mind takes them on board and manifests them. It is only once we have acknowledged this that we can see just how insignificant they are instead of the monsters that we allow them to become.

It is essential to do the following exercises in order to remove the fears once and for all.

EXERCISES

1) Make a list of the fears you have about not having money.
2) Make a list of the fears you have about having money.
3) CRUD these fears as follows:

   I RELEASE the fear that . . . . . .

   Three times.   Burn

VISUALISATION

Close your eyes and relax . . . . Let yourself sink into your seat . . . . Take some deep breaths . . . . With every out breath feel yourself going deeper and deeper . . . . You are going to go on an inner journey to your abundance chamber . . . . See yourself going down a long dark passage.... you have a candle to guide your way . . . . there are many doors either side of this passage with identification plaques on . . . . When you reach a door marked "Abundance chamber", take a few moments to take in the door. Is it locked or bolted? . . . . Is there any evidence that it has been used recently? . . . . Notice how you feel about entering this room . . . . Open the door using whatever you need to break through any locks or barriers . . . . What do you see when you go in? . . . Is it light or dark? . . . . Is it attractive or not taken care of? . . . . There is a cupboard in this room that contains all your fears about abundance . . . . How do you feel about opening that cupboard and facing these fears? . . . . What do you think they will be like? . . . . Go to the cupboard now and open it . . . . What is inside? . . . . Beside the cupboard there is a bonfire of etheric purple flames . . . . Throw everything that is in the cupboard onto the flames and see them transmute into divine love . . . . This transmutation creates a huge amount of pure white light that begins to transform the whole chamber . . . . See it become very beautiful . . . . See lovely items appear . . . . Windows with beautiful vistas . . . . In the centre of the room there is a treasure chest . . . . In this chest lies a symbol of your abundance . . . . Check out whether the chest is locked and then open it . . . . What is inside? Take your own personal symbol out of the chest . . . . See if there is any rubbish in this chest, if so, clear it out now by throwing it onto the etheric bonfire of purple flames . . . . It is now time to leave this chamber, knowing you can return at any time to maintain it . . . . Go back to the corridor with the candle to light your way . . . . Return along that passage . . . . And when you are ready bring your attention back into the room.

EMOTIONAL BODY

Guilt

I have always thought that guilt is a totally useless emotion and yet many of us are slaves to it. I find that guilt is the result of some form of manipulation either from another person, a religion or from our own egos. If we have been brought up in a manipulative household, the chances are that guilt has become a habit. Even though we have grown up and moved away, we may still take on responsibility and guilt for every adverse thing that happens in our vicinity.

Guilt is a choice, the trouble is that we are often unconsciously choosing to have it and therefore don't realise that we can choose not to have it. In religions guilt, along with fear, are often the tools used to hold its members.

Guilt plays a large part in abundance because our society makes us guilty for having money and guilty for not having money. Parents are made to feel guilty all the time especially with teenagers who, due to peer pressure, feel they need expensive designer sneakers and clothes. If the parent says no they are made to feel guilty for ostracising their child from its peer group and if they give in they feel guilty for spending so much. This is a no win situation.

Where there is guilt there will also be punishment. They work hand in hand. What better way do we have of punishing ourselves than to deprive ourselves of all the good things that life has to offer?

Guilt will drain the joy out of any situation; it does not allow us to feel good about having or spending money. Whatever we do it will make us wrong.

We need to note where we feel guilty about money. Do we feel it every time we buy something for ourselves? Do we feel it when others buy us something? Do we feel guilty for having money when there are people starving in the world? Do we feel guilty for not earning enough to provide for our own or our family's needs? Do we feel guilty for needing government benefits? Do we feel guilty for living off someone else?

The secret here is to consciously choose not to be guilty. It is a decision we need to make in advance and then reinforce every time it rears its head. Just let it go.

I AM AN INNOCENT CHILD OF THE UNIVERSE.

EXERCISES

1) Make a list of who or what makes you feel guilty. How does this manifest?
2) In what way do you feel guilty about money?
   CRUD
3) Whenever you know you are going to spend money, prepare in advance not to be guilty.

JEALOUSY AND RESENTMENT

Jealousy and resentment are two very corrosive and destructive emotions. They eat us up from the inside and can make us very obsessive.

Jealousy often starts between siblings. No matter how fair a parent tries to be, a child will perceive that its brother or sister is getting more, whether this be more love, more attention or more things. Often this will set up a pattern of jealousy that will just be transferred to someone else in adult life. A jealous person will always be comparing themselves with others whether physically or materially. So this, of course, gives the ego a field day.

If we are jealous of someone's good fortune, we create a huge block to allowing in any good fortune of our own. Luck is not a random thing, it is attracted to those who are sending out positive vibrations. If we expect good fortune we will receive it. My mother is always winning at raffles and prize draws. She has probably accumulated thousands and thousands of dollars worth of prizes and money. This was not particularly because she really wanted the things and therefore willed it, but more a calm acceptance that she would win. Sometimes, if she had to leave a function early she would give her tickets to a friend and say that she would pick up her prize or prizes the next day and sure enough she would win. At these same functions I would hear numerous people say "I don't know why I bother to get tickets, I never win anything" and sure enough they don't. We make our own luck and good fortune.

If we recognise that we have a tendency towards jealousy, look for ways to begin to shift it. The only person who suffers in the long run is ourselves. We have to stop comparing ourselves to others, and looking for the inequalities of life because we will always find them. We can accept our lot as being perfect for what we are here to work with and learn. We can always change it by deciding to change our minds. We rejoice in what we have and above all rejoice in what others have. This rejoicing needs to be genuine, not just saying the words in order to cover up our true feelings, although that can be a starting point.

The newspapers, particularly the tabloids, are very bad about playing on our jealous feelings. These papers cannot just rejoice at someone's success, they have to dig up, or make up dirt, or in some way assassinate the character of that person in order to devalue their success. We all do the same in smaller ways. When someone seems to have talent or wealth or success, we need to look for the defects in order to feel better about ourselves. We will always find the defects but the only person we have devalued is ourselves.

Resentment works in a very similar way to jealousy. It is often created as a result of a perceived injustice. Once it has got a hold it is quite difficult to let go and like jealousy it eats us up from the inside. Forgiveness is the cure for resentment and it takes a very big hearted person to choose to let go of resentment and to bring in healing forgiveness.

EXERCISES

1) Make a list of people you are jealous of. Write a letter that you will burn to each of these people letting go any jealousy. Release them with love.
2) Make a list of all the people you are harbouring a grudge or have resentment for. Write a letter that you will burn, letting go all resentment and sending them forgiveness.

THE UNIVERSE IS THE SOURCE

We have seen already how most people on this planet have bought into the scarcity principle. This is the belief that there is not enough to go round and that the source of prosperity is the Earth's resources that are a dwindling and finite resource. This plays a large part in creating the sense of lack that most people experience. It is essential that we change this belief in order to bring in abundance as a natural state to those inhabiting the planet. The prosperity principle states that the Universe and only the Universe is the source and it is completely unlimited and infinite and therefore so is our abundance. If this planet is to survive it is essential that we take on this belief and act accordingly.

The Universe is completely unconditionally loving and his unlimited abundance is available to absolutely everyone. Just for the asking. It makes no distinction between colour, race or religion. Nor does it make any judgement as to the deserving of an individual or how much they should be allowed. Good people can have just as much as evil people. It is we who are fixated with deserving. Most of the time our egos will tell us that we do not deserve to have good things in our lives. It will happily create adverse situations such as pain, fear, self loathing with each of these reinforcing the belief that we do not deserve happiness, love and abundance. This is a belief that has to be globally changed in order to usher in the new order.

Our natural state is to be wealthy, not just a select few, but everybody. Our natural state is also to be happy and loving and yet I know of no one personally who has reached this state on a constant basis.

We will know when we are totally abundant when we reach the state where we don't have to give it a thought. It is just totally natural and it is there all the time. To give an example of how this would be, compare it to breathing. We never give a thought as to whether there will be enough air for our next breath, it is just there and we breathe without thinking about it or trying to control it. We can't see the air and we just trust the process that the trees and plants are manufacturing enough oxygen for our every breath. We are like a bunch of asthmatics, all fighting for breath, in fear and panic. There is no less air available to an asthmatic than to someone breathing normally, it is dependent on that body's ability to take it in. There is total abundance all around us but we do not allow ourselves to take it in. In the case of money, it would be like there was a bank hole in the wall open twenty four hours a day and available to every single person on Earth. Behind this machine would be an unlimited source of money that is replaced after every withdrawal. Whenever someone needed or wanted something they would obtain the money. There would be no greed, no hoarding, no need to steal, no jealousy and I think most people would choose an easy but simple life because there would be no need to prove ourselves to others. This is available to us right now, it is just waiting to be tapped into. It is like we are living in an abundant orchard and because everyone is looking down at the ground for their prosperity and, therefore, are all fighting for a few manky windfalls. We need only to look up to the source of those windfalls to find trees bulging with fruit.

Once we have accepted that the Universe is the source and that abundance is available to us at any time for every single thing we could possibly need or want. We can then look at the channels through which this abundance and money can reach us. Most people might consider that only a few of these channels are open to them and then only in limited degrees. For example, some people might believe that their only source of money is what they earn and if they looked realistically at their prospects, their earnings would never come to more than a certain amount. If this amount is not enough to enable that person to thrive abundantly, then that person would believe that abundance is out of their reach. This belief would create that reality. These limitations are imposed on us by society and ourselves and it is essential that we let go of any limiting thoughts as to where our money and abundance may arrive from. If we do that then suddenly we are opening up the possibilities of miracles that provide our abundance. We cannot plan it because the Universe works in mysterious ways and we need only be open to receive it.

Here are some of the channels that I have thought of but please add any others that you can think of.

Channels of Money and Abundance:

You can earn it.

You can win it.

You can find it.

You can be given it.

You can marry and receive it.

You can inherit it.

You can invent something.

You can make it.

You can take it.

You can manifest it from the ethers.

You can sell something.

You can barter for it.

You can get it as a result of investments.

You can be given it as a reward.

You can be given it by the government as benefits.

You can receive it as a result of an insurance policy.

You can pick if from nature's free harvest.

I do not advocate stealing or counterfeiting but this is how some people choose to receive their money.

It is imperative that we keep our own personal channels open from the source and then begin to see how abundance arrives in miraculous ways.

There is going to be a domino effect with this process because when a few people have opened up to unlimited abundance they will gladly be distributing abundance to those around them knowing that it does not in anyway diminish what is available to them and in turn those who receive it will tap into the unlimited abundance consciousness and pass it on and the ripples will spread and spread until it covers the whole world.

So once again, those of us who choose to do this whole heartedly are the vanguard for the rest.

VISUALISATION

Opening up the channel to the Source.

Sit and relax . . . . Take some deep breaths and feel yourself becoming more deeply relaxed . . . . With every in breath you are taking in the beautiful gold/silver light and with every outbreath you are letting go the inky darkness of negativity . . . . Open up your crown chakra at the top of your head and see a strand of light coming out of your crown and going up and up until it reaches the Source . . . . You can see this source as an unlimited orb of pure brilliant white light . . . . See this white light coming down like a funnel until it enters your body through your crown chakra . . . . See it travel down throughout your whole body and then

come out through your feet and down into the Earth . . . .
Right down into the centre of the Planet . . . . You have now
opened up the channel to the Source and if you choose, you
can receive unlimited energy from it . . . . It cannot be
diminished or lost . . . . When you are ready bring your
attention back into the room.

ASKING

ASKING FOR WHAT YOU WANT IS THE KEY TO RECEIVING IT.

There is a Universal Law of non interference. What this
means is that we have been given absolute free will and free
choice and our guides and teachers are not allowed to
interfere unless we specifically ask for it. I often think this
must be incredibly frustrating for them as they watch us
make our mistakes.

As we have already pointed out, the Universe is the
source of our abundance and it is essential that
we remember to put out to it our requests for what we want.
Even when we know this we often forget to ask. There is
unlimited help and assistance available to us for everything
and yet we perhaps use a minute amount of this. Our guides
are more than willing to help us to clear our blockages; we
would not be wasting their energy as that is what they are
there for.

We are often taught as children that it is not polite to
ask. We have to wait until we are offered. This having been
drummed into us, many people have a real problem with
asking as an adult. Whether it is for a favour from a friend
or in a shop with assistants standing round, some people will
hunt for ages for what they want rather than just ask.

Also, if we still see money as being unspiritual or that we are being greedy and selfish in wanting our needs met, we are hardly going to turn to the Universe and ask him to give us what we want.

It is often said, "Be careful what you ask for because you might get it". This happened to someone I know. She really needed eight thousand pounds for something so she asked for it and programmed for it with visualisations etc. and a few weeks later she was burgled. Luckily she was insured and when the cheque came through it was for eight thousand pounds. She realised that in asking she had not made any provisos. When I ask I usually add the proviso, "if it is in my highest good". From our perspective we cannot see the whole picture and therefore we cannot tell whether what we have asked for is for our good or our detriment.

I suggest asking each day. When you wake or get up say something like:

I ASK FOR MY NEEDS AND DESIRES TO BE TAKEN CARE OF ABUNDANTLY THIS DAY AND I OPEN MYSELF UP TO RECEIVE AS LONG AS IT IS FOR MY HIGHEST GOOD AND THE GOOD OF ALL MANKIND.

MY CUP RUNNETH OVER

The symbol that I have been given for abundance is that of a chalice that is overflowing all the time with abundance. This abundance is not just money but love, joy, laughter, creative and personal fulfilment, happiness, contentment, peace, harmony and wisdom. At the bottom of this chalice is a limitless supply of all these things and whenever any is used it is immediately replaced.

Because we are taught that money is a limited commodity, every time we spend money we see our supply dwindling and therefore either feel guilt or do not enjoy it as much as we might. Even though we have gained in that purchase we have also lost because that money is no longer available to spend on something we might find we need or want more. This is all part of our scarcity consciousness. A friend of mine decided to take three of her grandchildren away to her caravan for a little holiday. She did not have much money to spare so she decided how much she could afford to spend on them for treats and toys. She explained to them a few times how much money was available and that they could choose what it was spent on. When it was gone it was gone. This did not get through to the children who spent the money in the first couple of days and then wanted more. My friend said there wasn't any more and they insisted that because she still had money in her purse that there must be. I think she felt a sense of disappointment that the holiday was dominated by their demands and wrangles over money and that they were being materialistic rather than being willing to enjoy nature and pursuits that were enjoyable and free. However, if we look at this, these children were prosperity conscious, they believed that money came from a limitless source that could not be diminished. They were young enough to know that our natural state is to be abundant. It was my friend who was actually stuck in the scarcity consciousness and she was teaching the children to be the same way. In order for them to have their abundant beliefs confirmed my friend would have needed to be in a position to be the intermediary of those unlimited funds.

To illustrate this. Imagine we are given a jug of water and are told that this is our share of the abundance pool and when it is gone there is no more. Think of the consequences of this. It would create a good deal of fear because we would worry about how we would survive once this commodity ran out. We would feel guilt every time we took a drink because there would be less there. We would become obsessed with it, making sure we didn't waste any or protecting it from someone trying to steal it. We would allow ourselves pain and suffering or dehydration rather than take too much from this dwindling resource. Alternatively, imagine we are given the same jug of water and were told that when we have finished it that there is a fountain that never runs dry where we could fill it up from. The consequences of this would be that we would drink our fill whenever we wanted it. We would get on with important aspects of our lives without worrying about our next drink. Every time someone came round we would invite them to drink as much as they wanted, we would be free of worry and fear of dying of thirst. Life would be simpler and more fulfilling.

The only difference in these two scenarios is that in the first one we were told that this was all there is and in the other we are told that there is an unlimited source that could be tapped into at any time. The jug was just the vessel that enabled the water to get to us. This is exactly what happens to us in childhood. We are taught that there is only a limited amount of available money. Phrases like "You must learn the value of money", "Money doesn't grow on trees", "Do you think I am made of money" get bandied about. By the time we reach adulthood, scarcity is firmly imprinted in our conscious and unconscious minds and we then pass it on to our children and so on. It is absolutely essential that we stop the rot now and change this very destructive belief.

Most of us have created patterns of behaviour with money. There is an upper level that we allow into our lives. For most people this is their monthly or weekly wages. There is also a lower level that we allow our money to dwindle to before it gets replenished. Some people always like to keep something in reserve, others spend down to the last penny while others will go into overdraft each month. This pattern seems to get set in the unconscious after a while and is hard to break out of. Even when we try to save a bit extra one month, an unexpected bill will appear and eat it all up. It is important that we consciously begin to break our money patterns and start to see that our money does not need to diminish every time we spend it. When we spend money, we can affirm that it is immediately replaced so that our supply does not diminish. I had been talking about this to a group of friends and how to visualise our purses filling up with the money we spent plus interest. We all went out to supper after a talk and when it was time to pay the bill which, for one friend, was around nine pounds, she found a ten pound note she didn't know she had hidden among her cards in her purse.

Once we can start trusting the flow of money energy returning to us, we can then allow that flow to extend to others. It is like when we are in an economic boom. Everyone benefits because we are all willing to spend our money freely knowing there is plenty more where that came from, therefore more money is in circulation. However, in a recession there is no difference in the amount of money available; that remains the same but people are fearful of losing their money, they hang onto it and nobody gains.

EXERCISES

1) The top of this chalice represents unlimited abundance, the bottom represents total scarcity. Draw two lines on the chalice. The top line represents the degree to which you allow abundance to come in. The bottom line shows the level to which your prosperity falls before it is replenished. If you go into overdraft draw the line on the stem of the chalice.

2) Note that these two levels have probably become a set pattern you may be stuck in.

3) Look at ways in which you can consciously begin to break this pattern.

4) Whenever you spend any money or write a cheque, immediately see it being replenished.

5) Put a note in your purse and cheque book saying:

I HAVE AN UNLIMITED SOURCE OF ABUNDANCE. WHENEVER I SPEND ANY MONEY IT IS IMMEDIATELY REPLACED WITH INTEREST.

ENERGY

ENERGY IS THE KEY TO HEALING

In its essence money is just energy. We put onto money a great deal of emotional and mental baggage that means that we lose touch with what it is really about. Money has the same properties as any energy and like any other energy it needs to move and flow, it does not like to be stagnant or blocked. If it were left to its own devices it would flow naturally and effortlessly but we have put obstacles in its way. These blockages are many and various and they include negative mental beliefs, fears, family patterning and so on. Unless these blockages are removed this money energy cannot flow. This is why it is so important to identify and remove these blockages. We don't need to do anything consciously to make the energy flow because it will do it naturally once the barriers are removed.

Energy has different frequencies and depending how high or low the frequency is that energy will manifest itself in different ways. Colour, sound, light, shape are all different frequencies of energy. The lower the frequency the more dense the energy becomes. So things that we can touch are vibrating less frequently. Everything on this planet is made up of energy vibrating, including ourselves. We are able to vibrate at hugely varying frequencies and one purpose we have on earth is to raise our vibrations. The higher our vibrations are the closer we become to our Divine selves, the lower the vibration, the more we are relating to our ego selves. When we are at a low vibration life becomes much more of a struggle because of the denseness of the energy. It feels like we are wading through treacle and we are often exhausted by the effort. The higher our vibration becomes the lighter everything is. Everything becomes easy and effortless. It doesn't mean that we stop being presented with lessons to learn but we are able to see them for what they are and therefore deal with them quickly.

Regarding money, therefore, if we have seen money as a negative force and we work hard to raise our vibration, we are then repelling money rather than drawing it to us. If our vibration is low and we see money as being the thing that will make things right, we are still repelling it. Seeing money as a negative force is an ego ploy that has had a great effect for many people. Money is just an energy, it is neither positive or negative until we put our judgements onto it.

MAGNETISM

We have an electromagnetic force field around us as does the Earth and the living things upon it. The strength of this force field can vary greatly, many being undetectable by modern technology.

As with a magnet there are two opposing polarities; we see these polarities as being positive and negative. Like will attract like and it will repel the opposite polarity. Therefore when we are putting out a positive vibration we will magnetise to us positive people and situations, equally when we are putting out negativity we will magnetise negativity. These negative and positive energies are made up of thoughts, beliefs and emotions. None of us are all negative or all positive, we are all a mixture of the two. However, whichever side comes out on top will decide whether we have a positive or negative magnetic force field.

One of the problems we have with changing our negatives into positives is that once again most of them are unconscious. If we ask ourselves what our last thought was, rarely will we be able to remember it and it might have taken place only one second ago. So thousands and thousands of thoughts will occur every day without our even being aware of whether they were positive, negative or neutral. These thoughts will have been fuelled by our beliefs and emotions. When we are feeling angry our thoughts will be extremely negative and not just towards the situations or person that triggered the anger. Therefore, in order to make sure that our unconscious thoughts are not negative it is essential to release the negative beliefs and emotions.

Many people use affirmations in order to help change negative patterns. An affirmation is just a positive statement. Some people have become slightly disillusioned about affirmations after using them religiously for a few weeks and not seeing any results. The reason for this is simply that the negative thoughts still outnumber the positive. Each affirmation will, in effect, cancel out one negative thought or statement. Only when we are in credit will we begin to notice a change in our lives. If we are only slightly in credit, the magnetic force field will be low and consequently will be too weak to attract a huge amount of bounty to us. As it gets stronger it will be pulling in positivity to us quicker and from further afield. We will become an irresistible force to anything that is vibrating on a similar frequency to our own.

A tip with affirmations is to find one that is easy to remember and say, not too long or complicated, then say it almost like a mantra at times during the day when we don't need to engage our minds. Like while driving or hoovering or exercising. A good general affirmation to use is: "I LOVE MYSELF UNCONDITIONALLY". We can keep repeating it until we are saying it in our minds and it almost becomes automatic. The benefits of this are two-fold. First, every time we say it we are clocking up positives and secondly if our minds are engaged saying positive statements, it cannot be saying negative ones. I find this technique particularly useful when a negative situation has occurred, something traumatic or a row perhaps. Usually we find negative thoughts going round and round in our heads until we nearly become demented with them. Start saying an affirmation mantra until the thoughts disappear.

Another pitfall with positive and negative thoughts is that often we don't recognise when a thought is negative. We all enjoy a good moan, gossip or bitch every now and then but we can clock up a good few negatives while indulging in these pastimes and the end result of it can be quite detrimental to ourselves.

Remember also that if we become aware that we have had a negative thought or said a negative statement, we can withdraw it by cancelling it and then saying an affirmation that puts us back in credit.

EXERCISES

1) Everyday take 5 minutes to monitor your thoughts and CANCEL any negative ones and say an affirmation.

2) Find out each day whether your negative thoughts out number your positive by blanking your mind and asking your unconscious mind the percentage of negative thoughts as opposed to positive you have had in the previous 24 hours.

3) If the percentage is above 50 you know what to do.

TRUST

TRUST IS THE KEY TO ABOLISHING WORRY

Trust is an essential part of the path to abundance. Where there is worry and fear there is no trust. Worry and fear are usually about something that may never happen. They are often a figment of our imagination, but we get so caught up in this negative fantasy that we begin to believe that it's the truth.

Trust realigns us to our Divine selves and consequently draws to us what we need at any given time. The Universe wants us to be abundant, it doesn't want us to spend all our energy just surviving. Trust sets off a belief that everything is taken care of and if this belief becomes firmly anchored in the unconscious, that is exactly what is going to manifest in the physical. The only part of the process that needs to be conscious is the trust. I find an area of life where I use trust is when I am travelling to an appointment. If, before I leave, I affirm that I trust that I will arrive at my destination at exactly the right moment, then I can relax and enjoy the journey and even if I am late I usually find that the person has just got in, or for some reason it suited them that I was delayed. If I forget to trust this, I often find that the journey is very fraught. If I run into traffic which, in London is inevitable, I get very uptight, frustrated, irritable and reach my destination exhausted and stressed.

Trust is an ongoing process, it is not enough to do it once and then either think that that should do it forever or then think that it doesn't work. Trust is a very powerful thing but it is an active process. It is like cleaning our teeth, we have to do it every day to really notice the difference. It is also like a muscle that needs constant exercise, if a body builder doesn't work out regularly, the muscles begin to grow flabby. Someone in one of my groups, (while we were doing the abundance plan) worked on actively trusting even though she was going to have a difficult month financially because her husband was in the middle of changing jobs and there would be no income until the end of the month. They managed without getting into fear and worry and the first pay cheque came through and then out of the blue they won a computer worth two thousand pounds, which they all needed. There was a sense of euphoria and a feeling of confirmation that it actually worked. Because they felt they had cracked it, they let the trust slide and within a couple of weeks, all the old fears and worries returned and within a few days they were summoned to the bank. **TRUST IS AN ONGOING PROCESS.**

Trust is not a question of just saying an affirmation or a few words, we do need to put the belief and intention behind it, that everything is taken care of at a higher level. It is also important that we allow our higher selves to know what is best so that we don't try and manipulate it. Just as when I go out to an appointment I trust that I will get there at whatever time is best, this is not necessarily the time that was arranged.

Real trust acknowledges that nothing is ever wrong. No matter what happens it is happening for a good reason that perhaps we are not able to see at this precise time but which becomes evident further down the line. This became illustrated to me when I was attacked at five in the morning at my London flat. This was probably the best thing that could have happened to me although it didn't feel like it at the time. I immediately moved to the country and have met a wonderful new circle of friends and away from the dense negativity of London and my work was able to take off. If we can bring this philosophy into our lives, it sets us free.

We are able to accept everything that happens knowing that ultimately it is beneficial to us. There is no worry, no blame to the self or others, no sense of being let down or a victim and this can be a wonderful feeling.

Once we trust that something has been taken care of we can begin to act as if it has happened already. This reinforces the trust and also speeds up the process because our unconscious will then hurry to catch up with us and manifest it.

FAKE IT UNTIL YOU MAKE IT.

Do not try and manipulate trust because then we block it. We can leave the whys and wherefores up to our higher selves. **JUST TRUST AND LET GO.**

EXERCISES

1) Place a card or a piece of paper with a reminder to actively trust, somewhere where you will see it each morning. Perhaps on the bathroom mirror or on your hairbrush.

2) My version would be:

I TRUST THAT EVERYTHING TODAY IS TAKEN CARE OF, FOR THE HIGHEST GOOD OF ALL MANKIND.

NEED

One of the main blocks to abundance is our need for it. A need is something that we perceive to be essential to our well-being that we do not have enough of. A need is usually created by what we did not receive consistently within our childhood. Tbis creates an illusion of emptiness, which no matter how much we get does not even begin to fill the void.

The main reason that a perception of need blocks abundance is that a need is always a lack of something. If we send out a message of lack to the Universe, it can only send the illusion of lack back to us. This in turn reinforces a sense of not having enough and also a complete powerlessness to get what we want. We are then in a state of struggle, which perpetuates our sense of lack.

There is something that I call the Divine conundrum. It states **IT IS ONLY WHEN WE PERCEIVE THAT WE ALREADY HAVE WHAT WE NEED THAT EVERY-THING BECOMES AVAILABLE TO US**. When this understanding kicks in, we actually find that when we can have anything, we only want the things that actively enhance our lives. The more we are able to have, the less we actually want. This means that we do not waste energy and resources that could be put to better use elsewhere.

When we are living and working with the Divine conundrum, it is interesting to note that what we need will usually be given to us before we are consciously aware that we need it. This will often be people, situations, books or information. There is a miraculous synchronicity at work here, which never ceases to amaze me. In a way we only discover what we need when it arrives. Using this understanding, we can actively acknowledge that whatever turns up in our lives is of some benefit to us though it may require some thought to discover what it is. I must stress here that this also applies to the more challenging or traumatic things that life throws at us. We simply ask ourselves what we need from this situation. It may be the catalyst to putting us back on course or the obstacle to prevent us from going further down a dead end alley.

There is another area of need that will effectively block abundance. **WHEN WE HAVE THE NEED TO EXPERIENCE OURSELVES IN TERMS OF THE MATERIAL, WE PREVENT UNLIMITED ABUNDANCE FROM COMING INTO OUR LIVES.** When we want to present who we are by what car we drive or our house or clothes or the things that we have, we are unable to access who we truly are. Our higher selves are the source of our abundant energy and not the physical selves. Once again where there is a need, it becomes nigh on impossible to consistently meet it. Whatever things we have will not make us feel good enough so we will look to more and more things to give us this positive self-image. This then becomes a vicious cycle that is hard to break out of.

There is another aspect of this pattern where we think that at least if we have fooled other people into thinking that we are good enough and are getting our needs met, then it is easier for us to deal with our own sense of inadequacy. Our lives then become about putting on the show and living a superficial cardboard cut out existence instead of finding the real substance underneath and healing any illusions that are preventing us from having a truly abundant life.

EXERCISES

1) What needs do you have that are not being consistently met?

2) Do you devote time and energy to trying to get these needs fulfilled?

3) Are you constantly focused on what you don't have or can't afford rather than on what you do have?

4) Begin to bring in the understanding that everything you have in your life right now is exactly what you need, even if it is only there to show you the reflection of how you are creating lack in your world.

5) Look for the gift in whatever life presents you withy. It will always be there even in the most difficult or challenging situtation.

6) Stay in the moment and wait to see what turns up in order to see what your needs are.

7) Bring in and anchor the belief-

EVERYTHING I NEED AND WANT IS PRESENTED TO ME IN THE PERFECT MOMENT.

SURRENDER

SURRENDER IS THE KEY TO LETTING GO RESISTANCE

There has been a strong emphasis in recent years to make things happen rather than to allow them to happen. We have become very goal orientated. Very often these goals are what society deems to be necessary for success. Some people would manage to achieve these goals and often would wonder why this success did not make them happy, so they would then set a new goal in the hope that this would succeed where the others had failed. The vast majority fail to reach their goals. They have feelings of failure, of being useless. This would then contribute to feelings of low self-esteem and frustration. When we seek to control our lives, it is our ego minds that are in the driving seat and since our ego minds do not want us to feel inner peace, contentment or fulfilment. Achieving and striving towards goals will rarely create those results.

One aspect of life that is particularly exciting is following our inner knowing and going down a path where we do not know what the final destination or goal is. Yet we accept that where we are going is absolutely where it is best for us to be. When we allow our higher selves to guide our lives, it runs like clockwork. When our egos run our lives, we are forever being sent up blind alleys.

Since we cannot foresee the twists and turns that lie head for us on the path of life, we cannot plan for them. When we surrender, we are surrendering to our higher selves. It is like we hand over the remote control unit knowing that it will not be abused and trusting that our Divine selves knows which button to press at exactly the right time.

We surrender to our highest good, not knowing what that will be. This can set us free. We stop resisting what life is presenting to us and start flowing with the tide instead of swimming against it. This allows a great deal of energy to be available to us that previously had been taken up with resistance. This energy can then be more beneficially channelled into dealing with the challenges of life, easily and effortlessly.

EXERCISES

1) Be aware of situations and people that you are trying to control. Make a conscious effort to let go and allow these people and things to BE.

I SURRENDER TO MY HIGHEST GOOD.

BALANCING MALE & FEMALE

BALANCING MALE & FEMALE IS THE KEY TO WHOLENESS

Understanding the roles played by our male and female sides and seeing where the imbalances lie is an important aspect of our general growth but it also has a part to play in our abundance.

First of all I want to make it quite clear that when I talk about male and female, I do not mean men and women. Within each man and woman there ideally should be equal parts of male and female.

For thousands of years we have been living in a male dominated society where female traits have been repressed and even persecuted. It is estimated that over six million women were killed for witchcraft or related charges. Most of these women were just displaying their female strengths, like intuition, healing, nurturing, expanding consciousness and so on. They were killed because these powers were threatening to men who didn't realise that these female traits were lying dormant within themselves. As we have already mentioned, when women began to rise over the last few decades instead of trying to expand their female sides and begin to balance society, they tried to play men at their own game which brought in more male energy and further imbalance on the planet. This is changing very quickly as both men and woman are opening up to their female sides.

The female aspect is the link between the higher and lower selves. The female is the receiver, by this I mean that she houses the transmitter that is able to receive information from the higher self, from guides and teachers. This transmitter is what we call intuition. It may seem that intuition is a bit of a hit and miss affair, not to be relied on all the time. This is only because we are a bit rusty. If this ability is worked on and honed down it gives us total guidance and direction in any given moment. Life becomes much easier, we are not giving into the ego and its mind chatter. We keep on raising our vibration by not being bogged down by negativity. However, this only takes us so far because the female side is the passive side, it is the be-er not the do-er and in order to function on the Earth we have to ACT upon our intuition and this is where the male side comes in. This side is aligned to the left side of the brain and right side of the body. The left brain is the logical side, it is the problem solver and the right side of the body in most people is the stronger side, it is physically able to do more. So if we put this in a nutshell: the female side receives the guidance and instructions and she then tells the male side WHAT he needs to do and he then takes over and works out HOW he can best achieve this. Hence the phrase, "Behind every great man there is a great woman".

The problem with this has been that our inner world reflects our outer world. Just as our male dominated society has tried to suppress and destroy these female qualities, so has our ego dominated mind tried to do the same for reasons we have explained. If the ego can in effect, shut down the transmitter then the only guidance that person is listening to comes from the ego itself. This can then perpetuate the negativity and chaos that the ego thrives on. One of the ways the ego and logical male uses to shut down the female side is by using ridicule. I have found in my work that one thing people fear almost more than anything is embarrassment and humiliation, so this then can be a very powerful weapon. Scorn is poured on the intuitive practitioners, they are hailed as charlatans, mentally simple or weirdoes and are summarily dismissed. There may not be any physical persecution for those using and working with intuition but there is certainly a mental and emotional persecution going on right now.

Obviously imbalances occur on both sides and happen in various ways. I will mention a few of these that have come up in my groups. Notice if any of these relate to you. Where there is an excess of female (yin) energy with very little male (yang) energy to balance. The female energy is very passive, can be prone to abuse, has no confidence in itsself and consequently has shut down the transmitter. She finds it hard to make decisions let alone act upon them. Feels like a victim. Tries hard to please but often finds this creates the opposite effect. These people have often shut down their male side altogether and usually attract partners who are as extreme in their yang as they are in their yin. This is natures way of trying to create a balance but the result can be very destructive.

Equally, the person who has an extreme of male energy and has shut down the female may be a tyrant or a bully, looking for a victim. This person actually feels quite powerless and has to counteract this sense of weakness by trying to prove themselves physically powerful and by creating fear in others. This person will ooze aggression and if this is channelled into sport, or some other activity, it may prove very successful. Obviously these two examples are the extreme and most people fit somewhere in-between. Another scenario is when either the male or female side try to take on traits and qualities of the other without actually having the wherewiththal to carry it out. How this manifests is when the female side, having received the guidance, does not trust the male side to carry it out and therefore takes on an action role that she does not have the capabilities for. Therefore, in life, the ideas will have been good but they never quite make it into the physical. The opposite of this is when the male side tries to receive its own guidance by bypassing the female altogether. This guidance then comes from the ego, often well disguised so that this male side thinks it is from its higher self. Then when they act upon this guidance, it backfires because the source has not been pure. Yet another scenario is when both sides are strong but there is a problem with communication between these sides; this often results in a great deal of battling and frustration. Our imbalances will usually be reflected in our one to one relationships. If we are not in a relationship it might be that we have rejected either the male or female sides of ourselves. If we want to know where we are at on the inside, we need to look at what is happening on the outside and if we want to improve that relationship then there needs to be some shifts with our yin and yang.

So how does our balance of male and female affect our abundance and money? Once again, traditionally, money has been a completely male aspect of life. Men were expected to earn it and to decide how to spend it or save it. However, in our new way of thinking about abundance we know that the source of abundance is the Universe. We have also just stated that the female side is the bridge between the higher and lower selves, the bridge between Heaven and Earth, if you like. Therefore, as the female is the receiver, it is she who is going to be the one to manifest the abundance energy and then hand it over to the male side to anchor it in the here and now and to organise and manage it. Neither side can manage without the other, neither is more important, both are essential. This goes against any conditioning we have regarding money where the male is the provider, traditionally, and often the women are expected to manage household expenses out of a housekeeping budget. It is essential that we begin to redefine the roles of male and female and their attitudes to money. Again, I must stress that this is the male and female within all of us, whether we be male or female. Balancing our own male and female is such an important aspect of our growth. When we are whole and in balance we can then attract a life partner who is equally whole and balanced. If we are out of balance, we look to a partner to create that balance and if one or other in the partnership changes then an imbalance occurs that may create incompatibility and the relationship breaks down.

The following exercises are designed to help us to understand the aspects of male and female and to create a new sense of their purpose.

EXERCISES

1) In order to find out where your male/female imbalances are, blank your mind and ask your unconscious mind what percentage of male energy you have to female energy. Keep asking this until your subconscious gives you a figure.

If the percentage is over 50% then you have an excess of male (yang) energy and it needs to be balanced by bringing in more female (yin) energy. Equally if the percentage is less than 50%, then you need to bring in more male energy.

2) Write a letter to your female side, explain to her what her responsibilities are and how any imbalances need to be corrected. Set up the new order for prosperity and abundance in your life. Explain to your female side that from now on she will be the receiver of abundance energy and she will then pass it over to your male side in order to ground and manifest it. Explain the importance of communication between male and female.

3) Write a letter to your male side explaining his roles in your life and the importance of working in unity with the female side. Point out that the female side receives the instructions that she passes on to the male side to carry out.

4) The sideways figure of eight or infinity sign   represents the connecting and balancing of the right and left brain. Draw this symbol either on paper or in the air as often as you can. This will help unify the male and female sides.

SELF WORTH

SELF WORTH IS THE KEY TO PROSPERITY

Everything in our lives is a reflection of our inner selves and consequently the degree of worth we give to ourselves is the degree that the Universe then reflects back to us. This is the amount of prosperity we let into our lives. To raise this prosperity, it is not about working harder, or getting more qualifications but raising our self-esteem.

Our self-esteem or self-worth is usually set in fairly early childhood. It is given or taken away from us by our parents and those who are around and have an influence on us. This may be the extended family, or a child minder or nanny. The most scandalous thing is that there are no classes in parenting for males and females. The only example we are given of parenting is that given us by our own parents and this is often totally dysfunctional. We will either repeat our parents' patterns or we will react against them and go to the opposite extreme which can be just as detrimental.

Getting the balance right in parenting has got to be the most difficult job in the world. It is hardly surprising that very few people manage to achieve it. Babies and children learn who they are by gauging people's reactions to them, they have no sense of themselves. Children brought up with siblings will often be given labels, like, the pretty one, the clever one, the funny one, the creative one and so on. I have found that once given this label they almost think this is all they have to offer as a person instead of seeing themselves as a whole rounded person. The pretty one may believe that she is stupid, and the clever one believes she is ugly and useless at anything that is not academic. This colours their whole world and they are often amazed to find out gifts in later life. Babies and children take their estimation of themselves more from people's actions than their words. Parents can tell a child how much they love it until the cows come home but if they are rarely there then that child will tell itself that there must be something very wrong with it that its parents don't want to be with them, therefore, they must be unlovable. When we leave a child with someone else to care for them, we have no idea what messages our children may be receiving unconsciously from that person that is going to seriously affect that child's self-esteem and self-worth. Even within a family, children can be getting very different messages from their parents' behaviour. A good child in a big family can often be ignored simply because he or she is not getting any attention as the parents time is taken up by those demanding attention. That child would certainly get the message that he or she was worth less of its parents time, so it was worth less altogether than its siblings.

There is an astounding amount of abuse that is now coming to light and the legacy of this is a great deal of low self-esteem. Even when the perpetrator of the abuse is not one of the parents, there is often a sense that the parent failed to protect them or even recognise the problem after the fact. Therefore it feels like there is some collusion going on.

Often parents try to make up for their own deprived childhood with their children. They may project onto the child their own lack of confidence and low self-esteem when the child is actually quite balanced and secure. The parent may then bolster the child's confidence constantly and end up creating an imbalance. This can create in the child an over active ego that is not always responded to favourably outside the immediate family and consequently the child's self-esteem becomes eroded.

It is quite common for female children to get the message that the male of the species is superior and constantly take that belief into their adult life.

It is very important that we reprogram our beliefs about ourselves and realise how they have been created and what the reality was at the time. We can talk to our parents, ask about our childhoods and see what was going on in their lives at the time. Know that our parents did their best with the resources that were available to them at the time. Accept that as we chose our parents, we are in effect going to choose the particular set of challenges that our childhoods have created. How are we still manifesting those challenges in our lives? We can work on letting them go.

EXERCISES

1) Look at areas in your life that give you feelings of low self esteem. For instance.

Not intelligent enough

Not attractive enough

Not confident enough

Not rich enough

Not fit enough

Not popular enough

Not interesting enough

Not creative enough, etc.

2) Look at your list and see who or what made you feel or believe this about yourself. Make sure both parents are included.

3) Write a letter to each of these people telling them that this is not who you are and that you release any beliefs that you are this way. Burn them.

SELF LOVE

LOVE IS THE KEY TO EVERYTHING

Self love is greatly linked to self-worth. If we do not value ourselves then we certainly do not love ourselves. We talk a great deal about unconditional love and yet it is not something we often experience. The closest I have come to this is with my dogs. Dogs are past masters at unconditional love. No matter who we are, no matter how well or badly we treat them, they love us with absolute devotion. They accept us just as we are and have no expectations.

If we don't love ourselves unconditionally then we can't love someone else unconditionally. We then expect other people to love us when we are unable to and even when they do we often find it hard to believe and so we then test them and their love all the time.

Learning to love ourselves is probably the most important thing we can do. If we love ourselves then we are happy to give ourselves everything that is good for us. Good health, joyful relationships, happiness, fulfilment and **ABUNDANCE**. If we do not have these things then we do not love ourselves enough to give them. All these things and more are well within our power to achieve if we choose to. It is self love and self love alone that allows us to make those choices. We need to decide to love ourselves and then begin to moderate our behaviour to show that we do love ourselves. This means becoming conscious of our actions and just checking within to see if this action is self loving or self destructive. This is a gradual process that will begin to change as long as we have the discipline to keep on being conscious. As we learn to love ourselves more, the benefits are soon felt, we attract loving people and situations to us that then increases our well being.

There are many things that stand in the way of unconditional self love. One of these is the ego. The ego constantly feeds us unloving thoughts about ourselves. If we listen to and believe what the ego tells us, we will find it virtually impossible to learn to love ourselves. The trick is to listen to our thoughts and if they are unloving then it is necessary to cancel them and reprogram loving thoughts. Another block to self love are various shadow selves that we have. These have formed due to our own personal circumstances and they need to be brought into the light and aligned with our Divine self. The Divine only gives us positive and loving thoughts.

As I have stated, this is an exceedingly important area on which to work. The amount of abundance we allow in will increase as our love of self increases. As self love increases so will our ability to love others. Relationships will then be based on pure love and not on need and dependency. Absolutely every area of life will improve immeasurably as we bring in more self love.

EXERCISES

1) Write a list of the qualities that you love or like about yourself.

2) Write a list of the qualities you dislike about yourself. Look at the qualities you dislike about yourself and see if you can change your perception of these qualities and learn to like them. If this is impossible then look at ways in which you can change yourself.

3) Write a love letter to yourself. Tell yourself all the things you love and appreciate about yourself. (This is not big-headed and will not be read or judged by other people, so go to town.)

4) Monitor your thoughts. If they are not loving then CANCEL them and say:

I LOVE MYSELF UNCONDITIONALLY.

SELF ANGER

RELEASING ANGER IS THE KEY TO FORGIVENESS

As we mentioned in the previous chapter, one of the blocks to self love are various shadow selves. We will call these shadow selves, sub-personalities. These sub-personalities have been created by various circumstances in our lives. Some of these sub-personalities maybe tyrannical, they will possibly have formed due to the influence of people in our lives with those characteristics. They may be members of the family or teachers. The effect of this may seem like housing a couple of Hitlers inside us. Equally, some of our sub-personalities may be in victim mode. Each of these sub-personalities have qualities that are extremely positive but because they are angry with us or we are angry with them, these qualities remain hidden.

We all experience self anger every day. When something untoward happens, we spill the milk or get stuck in traffic we direct our anger and frustration against ourselves. Often we manifest that anger by doing something that is detrimental to ourselves, like overeating, drinking, taking drugs, for instance. Once the pattern of anger against the self has been set, it becomes automatic and unconscious and it is extremely destructive. Even when we are conscious of this process and are given a choice, the anger is so deep seated that we will often choose the unloving option rather than the loving one.

Those who have been victims of abuse tend to have higher levels of anger against the self. This abuse could be physical, sexual, mental or emotional. It is almost as if the victim takes over where the abuser left off. This pattern of self-destructive behaviour will carry on until the person takes active steps to change this.

As with anything that is negative, if we expose it to the light it becomes transformed. In the following visualisation the sub-personalities that are angry with you or that you are angry with are brought into the light and transformed.

I suggest that you do this visualisation until all angry sub-personalities have been transformed.

VISUALISATION

Relax in your chair and take some deep breaths . . . . Let everything go . . . . With every out breath you become more deeply relaxed . . . . You are going to go on a journey to discover those sub-personalities that are holding anger to or from you . . . . High above your head you see a large sphere of white light . . . . See a column of light coming down from that sphere and totally surrounding you . . . . Take a few moments to take in the feelings you get from this light . . . . You are now going to be raised up this column of light as if it were a lift . . . . When you stop, step out of the column . . . . You see ahead of you a wooded area filled with little huts . . . . Each of these huts houses a sub-personality that is angry with you or that you are angry with . . . . Go towards the hut nearest to you . . . . You are perfectly safe, they cannot hurt you . . . . Knock on the door and observe as this sub-personality opens it . . . . What form does it take? . . . . Is it human or animal or some abstract form? Does it resemble someone you know? Go into the hut, notice whether this personality is angry with you or are you angry with it or perhaps you are both angry . . . . Express the anger or allow it to be expressed . . . . Do not hold back . . . . Get rid of it all . . . . When all the anger has been verbalised . . . . Take this sub-personality out of the hut and into the sunlight . . . . See a strong beam of light surround this sub-personality and as it touches it see it transform totally . . . . It may completely change form or just shed its negativity . . . . Give it a big hug and tell it that you love it . . . . Allow it to express its love for you . . . . See both of you surrounded by a beautiful pink light . . . . Notice what positive qualities this sub-personality now has and ask that these qualities be integrated into your being . . . . Take your sub-personality back to the hut that is now also transformed . . . . Whatever is needed to help this part of you in its purpose is now provided . . . . Bid this sub-personality a fond farewell and come out of the hut . . . . Repeat this process for two other sub-personalities then return to the column of white light and step into it . . . . Come down and into your body . . . . When you are ready bring your attention back into the room.

SELF ACCEPTANCE

ACCEPTANCE IS THE KEY TO HAPPINESS

The media and society are constantly giving us stereotypes that we are supposed to fit into. The most obvious of these involves our physical appearance. The powers that be have proclaimed a certain face and figure to be the ideal, the fact that almost no one can fit that ideal has led to a great deal of low self-esteem and self-destructive behaviour. In times gone by when the media was limited to reporting very dry political statements, there was not this negative obsession with our appearance and standards of beauty were very different anyway.

Many people are spending a great deal of time, energy and money trying to squeeze themselves into a box that was not made to fit them without realising that what they have is actually far better than what they are aspiring to. This does not just involve our physical appearance but lifestyles and personality traits and talents as well.

When we are preparing to enter a new lifetime we choose what traits and qualities we are going to have in our life. These are chosen carefully and are aligned with our purpose and mission on Earth. We are always given all the gifts and talents we need in order to fulfil our mission. Therefore, it makes very little sense to deny who we are and forever be striving to be someone else.

After birth we soon forget who we are and why we are here. Those who choose to bother may then spend a whole lifetime trying to remember. Each new self-discovery can then be assimilated into our lives.

Society puts a great deal of pressure on us to conform to the norm. We can control a flock of sheep that all do the same thing and blindly follow each other. The shepherd (society) can dictate where they go, what they do and, to an extent, what they think. However, it would take only one sheep to decide that it is an individual and that it is going to be and do what it decides, to create anarchy. The powerful weapon our society uses to keep us in line is ridicule. Society tells all the obedient sheep to laugh at the one that is not conforming or to tell it that it is weird and mad. Many people faced with this scenario will very quickly step back in line and it is fear of ridicule that will prevent many people from stepping out of line in the first place.

If we are not going to be trying forever to conform to an idealised clone then we need to recognise our own unique individual gifts and abilities. Note that if we have chosen these specific gifts and talents it is because we need to use them for our purpose on Earth.

Once we have recognised who we are then we need to allow ourselves to **ACCEPT** ourselves no matter how different we are from those around us. This is a very important phase because if we do **NOT** accept who we are then neither will those around us. They will act as the mirror of our non-acceptance. When we are comfortable with who we are then others are too and we can actually help them in their own transformation without uttering a word.

When we accept ourselves just as we are then we can also love ourselves. We cannot genuinely love ourselves if we are not happy with who we are. I want to stress here that there is nothing we have to change except our perception. We are already perfect just as we are.

When we are in a state of non-acceptance we are always fighting against ourselves. We will compare ourselves with someone else and believe that if only we had what they had, we would be all right.

Please note that when we do choose to step out of the line and become our own individual self, we do not need to become evangelical and broadcast it from the roof tops. It is an inner process and if kept as such, we do not need to expose ourselves to ridicule or, indeed, to any comment at all. We will also find that we are drawn to people who have also stepped out of line and, therefore, this can become the norm for us.

Sometimes, in order to get where we want to go, it is important to accept where we are now without fighting against it. For instance, we are working towards being totally abundant but if we fail to recognise the degree to that we are not abundant and then accepting this state of affairs without resistance or illusion then we are blocking ourselves from actually becoming it.

When we can **ACCEPT** that where we are on our path is exactly where we are meant to be, then the road ahead becomes clear and exciting.

EXERCISES

1) When you find yourself wanting to become something else or to conform to an ideal. Say three times.

I LOVE AND ACCEPT MYSELF JUST AS I AM.

COMMITMENT

Until there is commitment there is no real foundation to a project, a relationship or an aspect of growth. Most things start out as an idea or a thought and the thing that allows that idea to manifest in the physical is commitment.

As a general rule we are very indecisive. We fluctuate from one extreme to another, one minute thinking we want something and then the next minute finding reasons why it wouldn't be such a good idea. We all also indulge in wishful thinking, fantasising and daydreaming. "Wouldn't it be nice if...". For most of us these remain as fantasies because they are missing an essential ingredient to bring them into reality. We have stated that our thoughts and beliefs create our reality whether it is done consciously or unconsciously, so why then do these daydreams not come true if that is the case. As I have said we have many thoughts which are conflicting so a positive thought is often immediately cancelled out by a negative one. As in "Wouldn't it be nice if I won the lottery," is cancelled out by "You never win anything so why would you win the lottery?".

The Universe is a wonderful mirror, it sends us an accurate reflection of where we are at. If we are needy or living with a sense of lack, the Universe will send us lack, if we are sending out vibrations of abundance and prosperity then that is exactly what we get. We are either committed to lack or committed to abundance. Admittedly that commitment is often an unconscious one. In order for the Universe to send us back what we say we want there needs to be some sense of clarity. If our thoughts and beliefs do not back up what we say we want then the mirror becomes very cloudy and confused and confusion is often what we then get back. We get mixed messages, one minute seeming to say one thing and then the next minute the opposite. When we become committed to something we can then clear away the dross around that decision. It brings in a sense of focus and clarity to our lives. It points us in a certain direction that simplifies our choices and therefore our lives. The image we send out to the Universe is so well defined that it is able to send back exactly what is sent out. The Universe does not judge anything, it is just a mirror, so if something is not good for a person it doesn't then decide not to support it. Just as when sending out an image of lack, the Universe will send lack, if that image is for extreme wealth the Universe will not say "that wouldn't be very healthy for that person so I won't send it". We have all seen examples of people who are committed to having money and as a result of that commitment seem to have a Midas touch. Every deal they pull off amasses them millions. These people may be unscrupulous, immoral or crooks or they might be kind and loving. There is no council who decides whether they are deserving or not. All they needed was the commitment to be wealthy.

All we need is the commitment to abundance. This is not going to turn us into a hard nosed wheeler dealer but it is going to allow the Universe and our unconscious mind to do what they need to do to attract abundance into our lives.

When a dream remains pie in the sky, we will not receive it. Commitment anchors that dream into the here and now. There is only the present, if we program something into the future, the unconscious mind, which only deals in the now, will put that request into a file to be dealt with at a later date that never comes because the future is always in the future. This is why affirmations should always be put into the present tense.

When we commit to something, we give it energy, make a plan for it. For me commitment is like planting a seed that, if nurtured and watered, will blossom into whatever it is we desired.

In order to bring abundance into our lives, it is necessary to have a level of commitment in order to achieve it. When the commitment is there then miracles will take place. It is the first step that we need to take down the path of abundance.

EXERCISES

1) Make a list of the things you say you want.
2) Examine that list and with each want, ask yourself how committed you are to each desire. Write down on a scale of one to ten the level of commitment.

   If the level is less than 5, look at whether you really want this thing or what resistance you have to receiving it. Use other exercises in the book to remove the blocks you have to what you want.
3) Write a declaration of commitment to what you want to create in your life.

I . . . . (name) do solemnly declare my commitment to . . . .
4) End with **AND SO IT IS** and sign.

DO WHAT YOU LOVE

Many people believe that their only source of prosperity comes from their work. Society also tells us that in order to get a good, well paid job we need to be intelligent, we need to have good qualifications, bebsingle minded ambition and we need to work very hard. This discounts ninety percent of the population straight away. Other people may settle for a job at whatever level they believe they are capable. The purpose of this job is to pay the mortgage or rent, bills and food and hopefully to have enough left over for a holiday and a bit of leisure and social activity. Most of these people will be spending at least eight hours a day doing a job which, at best, is routine or stressful and, at worst, that they absolutely hate and yet they fear to lose it. It is certainly a crazy world where there is an expectation that we spend half our waking life doing something we don't like. My own mother demonstrated this to me after I had catered a large party for her. She said that I should go in for catering professionally; I told her that I would hate to do that and she immediately turned round and said, "Well we all have to do things we hate in order to earn a living". I thought about this and realised for how many people this belief was true. I also realised that I was certainly not going to buy into that mass belief.

The things we love to do are usually things that get squeezed into leisure hours. These things are often creative, sporty or social. Very few people manage to make a living from their hobbies and when they do it is rarely an abundant living and often the pressure to produce enough to sell enough to make enough to live on means that the initial joy and fulfilment of that creativity gets lost and the person ends up swapping one rat race for another.

There is a huge prejudice towards people being paid well for doing something they love. It is as if that love should be payment enough. We have been brainwashed into believing that work is not something to be enjoyed and there needs to be a great deal of fear keeping people in jobs they dislike. Fear of poverty, fear of having the house repossessed, fear of never finding a new job. Fears that we are too old, young, underqualified, overqualified, fat, thin, skilled, unskilled, to get whatever job we may want. This brainwashing has certainly worked because no one escapes. It is in society's interest to fuel these fears, to have a work force that is insecure and more easily controlled by believing the false propaganda that is spread around. We can find this in big companies that may spread a rumour that there are going to be widespread redundancies in a year's time. The object of this is to get the workforce to pull their socks up, fewer people go off sick, they may make an effort to increase productivity and bring in a competitive aspect to the work. Obviously the management think that they are benefiting from this situation. However, the downside of this can be disastrous to the people that the company depends on to make their profits. Morale becomes low, people are living with a sword of Damocles over their heads and the stress that is created from this can destroy marriages, break up families and have such a devastating effect on the physical body that can bring about an early demise. The cost to the human condition is incalculable and there seems to be no way out. It increases people's sense of being a victim to the system and being totally powerless.

I think the reason that the establishment felt that it was in their best interest to inject fear and imbalance into the work force is as a result of the sixties. This was a boom time and also a time of expansion in consciousness. People wanted to have a good time and there was the money to enable them to do this. Nobody wanted to do any of the low paid, menial jobs, so a work force of immigrants had to be imported in order to take on those jobs. When the boom was over, even a low paid job was better than none but now there was a whole strata of society fighting for jobs that a few years before no one would touch with a barge pole.

It is essential now that we start to shift our thinking away from work that is extremely bogged down with negativity. Fear, resentment, boredom, stress, insecurity, anger, geopathic stress, powerlessness and so on. All these things are very heavy and dense and, in effect, totally block the new prosperity energies that we need to tap into in order to move into the new abundant order. If we are in a job that we dislike, we are throwing a veil of darkness around us that makes it seem even harder to find a way out from under this heavy weight. When we love what we do then we put a bright and guiding light into our work that allows us to see where we want to go with it and that can increase our abundance. If we have a product or service that is infused with love then it will be attractive to people. Our customers will be drawn towards it without even knowing why on a conscious level. If a product has been created in an environment of fear, resentment, greed and boredom then it can become quite toxic to those who consume it.

We are all here upon this Earth with a purpose, a mission. We come into each lifetime knowing exactly what that mission is and we are all given the gifts, talents and wherewithal in order to achieve it. Then we promptly forget what it is and get bogged down with the human condition. We get lost by buying into our family and society's beliefs and conditioning. It's like we go through life with this thought nagging in the back of our minds, "I am sure I am meant to be doing something," but we get caught up in just surviving each day. In this lifetime most people reading this will have chosen to incarnate in order to aid and assist in the transformations that are going on on a planetary and human level. Therefore this lifetime is one of service both to the Earth and humanity.

Each person has their own particular area of service that they are wonderfully suited to and have the necessary attributes to carry it out. For many people these gifts have been suppressed and consequently may not have emerged yet. The essential ingredient in this life of service is love. This love works on many levels. First, we must love the manner in which we have chosen to serve. If we don't then perhaps we need to look again at our job. Do we need to change it or is there something blocking us from being able to bring that love in? Love also needs to be the primary message that we are trying to convey. Love heals and cures all and it is the one thing that can save the planet and those upon it.

We all have one single common purpose upon this Earth and that is to co-create Heaven on Earth. Both Heaven and Hell are on Earth, we have all probably experienced and contributed to Hell on Earth in our many lifetimes but now is the time to shift that. We all have a bright and beautiful light shining within us that is our Divine self. A baby is born with that light showing brightly, but gradually as we are exposed to the extremes of negativity that abound on the planet, veils of darkness begin to obstruct that light. How deeply we go into the negative condition is reflected in the number and thickness of these veils. For some people it appears as if the light has been extinguished altogether. This is not the case as every single person on the planet is a perfect shining being.

Our first job working towards our purpose is to remove the veils of darkness from our own shining Divine selves. This is an ongoing process but one that is quickly rewarded for as each veil is removed everything becomes lighter and we are able to see our way more easily. Once this process is well underway the next stage is to help others to begin to remove their veils of darkness and illusion. How we do this is up to each individual, everyone has their own unique abilities that decide their own personal work. For some this work will be paid, for others it may be voluntary but there does need to be energy coming to that person from one source or another otherwise there is burnout. The variety of jobs that can be done is unlimited. It may involve healing, communicating, teaching, networking information, inspiring people through music or dance, making people laugh, doing creative or artistic projects, leisure activities or whatever our gifts and enthusiasms dictate. What we choose to do is our **MINISTRY** and it is essential to stress that whatever our ministry is is crucial to making shifts on this planet. Some ministries will have a higher profile and will therefore seem like they are more important. This is NOT the case. If someone is shining their light they will have a profound impact on everyone they come into contact with. This person could actually change the life of someone they are standing next to in a bus queue without even speaking a word to them. It is always the ego that needs to compare and either tell us that our ministry is better or not as good as someone else's.

This ministry does not have to involve doing a job. I think that probably one of the most valuable jobs is to bring up healthy, happy, balanced children who have been allowed to remember who they are and what they are here for. So if we are a parent and that is our primary function, we don't think that we have to go out and become a politician in order to change the world. We only need to keep our light shining brightly.

It is important that we decide what our ministry is and then begin to expand it by increasing the love that flows through us for what we do and for those that are around us.

If we find ourselves in a job that we dislike then we have two options. First, we can change our perception of the job and learn to love it or we can change our jobs. If the first option is not easily achieved then it is a clear indication that we are in the wrong job anyway.

For many people their ministry will not be limited to just one thing. Our gifts and talents may be diverse and we are meant to use them or we would not have chosen them. It is important to have a flow of creative energy that can come from numerous activities. If we can obtain a balance between our various pursuits our level of fulfilment will be immense. Some things we do will involve a substantial output of energy while others will be energising and prevent us from becoming drained.

The reward for doing what we love is abundance. This occurs, not because we or the Universe decides that we deserve it for doing meaningful work but because when we bring love into our lives it dissolves the darkness and allows abundant energy to flow through.

EXERCISES

1) Write a list of the qualities, talents and gifts you have. (You may need others to help you identify them.)

2) Write a list of qualities, talents and gifts that you would like to have (regardless of likelihood).

3) Write a list of things you love to do.

How many of these things come into your ministry?

Look at ways that you can incorporate them into your life work.

4) Are you doing a job that you do not enjoy? If so . . .

5) Go inside and check out whether you can change your perception of the job or make changes within the job in order to learn to love it.

6) If you cannot learn to love what you are doing this is a clear indication that you need to make moves to change jobs.

7) Make a list of the beliefs you have about work and making a living.

8) CRUD the negative beliefs.

GRATITUDE

It is essential on our path to abundance that we recognise how much we have already and give thanks for it. We are so used to focusing on what we don't have and what we want but can't afford that we fail to appreciate how much we do have. Those reading this book probably would like to bring abundance into their lives. We rarely acknowledge every day how abundant we already are. If we focus on lack then that is what the Universe will appear to show us. However, if given the same circumstances we choose to see how very fortunate and abundant we are, the Universe will respond by showing us more.

I was sitting in a friend's living room and I looked around. She had a television and video, a nice music system, lovely decor and plants, comfortable furniture and central heating and yet by society's standards she comes into a very low income bracket. I realised how abundant she was in reality. This applies to virtually every household in the western world. These days everyone has phones, all mod cons, the easy availability of all foods under the sun. Yet how many people thank the Universe every day for all these things instead of moaning about the things that aren't right?

We all know how it is when we give a present to someone who is grateful and receives it with joy, we feel good and then want to give that person more. Alternatively, if we give a present to someone who appears to expect it or does not appreciate it, we then feel resentful and do not feel inclined to give them anything else. Perhaps this could be reflected on a bigger scale in our lives.

We are all fortunate enough to live on a stunningly beautiful planet, and yet do we appreciate it or take it for granted? There is such an abundance of beauty available to us. Even those who live in inner cities are only a bus ride away from glorious countryside rich with colour, wildlife and clean fresh air.

It is important that we bring a sense of appreciation and gratitude into our daily lives. Thank the Divine power for what we have and for all the beauty around we and it will respond by making more available to us.

EXERCISES

1) Make a list of all the things in your life that you are grateful for.

2) Write a letter to the Universe thanking it for all the good in your life.

NON-ATTACHMENT

I often find that people come up to me and say how they have done their affirmations every day and they do their visualisations and yet the thing they want hasn't come yet. They want to know where they have gone wrong. The fact is that there are probably many reasons for the blocks but one of them is that when we become attached to one particular outcome we create a block that prevents us getting what we need.

Control is a major issue for many people. The ego tells us that if we are in control of the people and situations in our lives then we are assuming power in our lives and therefore we cannot be a victim again. However, when we use control we are actually becoming a victim of our egos. Control is always saying that our egos know more than our Divine selves and it is therefore going to make happen whatever the ego decides is best. When this fails, which it often will, the ego mind will explain that this was because we were not exerting enough control so the next time, instead of seeing the control as the block, we end up trying to use more control. This is how a megalomaniac is created. Manipulation is another aspect of control, it is more subtle and is often harder to recognise and resist.

The importance of non attachment to an outcome is that it allows our higher self to assess what is in our highest interest and to find the best way to bring it into our lives. For instance, if someone was committed to increase abundance in their lives and a job with a greatly increased salary comes up and that person decides that that is the only way that they could get more money and as a result is determined to get the job. This creates a no win situation. The chances are that wanting the job too much may block it causing a feeling of failure and if that person does get the job and it is the wrong one for them and they have to do something they dislike, any enjoyment the added money gives is negated. The answer is to hand over the situation to our higher self, knowing then that our highest good is taken care of and we have a win-win situation. If we don't get the job, we win because it was not right for us and if we do get the job, we win because we know it is right. This handing over of control can change our lives dramatically for the better. It means that absolutely everything that happens to us is ultimately for our good and if we can trust that, it sets us free.

The break up of a relationship or loss of job happens to free us up for someone or something better, we then release ourselves from beating ourselves up for failure and are able to look forward to the unfolding of events. So program for the best and just allow it to happen instead of trying to make it happen.

Attachment to money is called greed. I think many people are confused about where prosperity ends and greed begins. We get such mixed messages about money and whether it is good or bad. Greed is the need to amass money in order to have a sense of power and superiority over others, it is an ego weapon. The person who has an attachment to the money will often spend very little money on anyone other than themselves. There is very little flow to this money and the main focus becomes obtaining more and more. John Paul Getty had pay phones installed in his home so that his guests did not sponge off him by making their phone calls while staying with him. Those who feel the need to save and store away a substantial amount of money are not necessarily being greedy. What they are showing is that they do not believe that the source of their money comes from an unlimited source. They therefore have the need to save for a rainy day or to put it away for their old age. When we plan for a rainy day we inevitably create one and often retired people are very fearful about dipping into their capital because they don't know if they may have a further ten, twenty or even thirty years.

The path to abundance is a letting go process. Very often we are obsessed about wanting something and then when we have got it, after the initial euphoria, we become totally disinterested and begin to fixate on the next thing. This happens when we have a belief that things are going to make us happy and feel good about ourselves. If we can let go our attachment to things, we are not saying that we are going to live a spartan existence without any belongings but as they assume less importance in our lives then we can concentrate our energies on the aspects of life that really do bring happiness and fulfilment.

EXERCISES

1) Write down anything that you feel you want very much
   but have not received. This can be material or
   something like a relationship, baby or a job.

VISUALISATION

Use this visualisation on each subject that you have just
written down.

Sit down and relax . . . . Take some deep breaths . . . .
With every in breath take in the beautiful gold/silver light
and see it spreading through your body . . . . And with every
out breath let go any negativity, see it as inky smoke emit-
ting from your mouth . . . . If it is something tangible then
give it colour and form . . . . If it is a situation or something
abstract then see a scenario unfold or give it a symbol . . . .
Put a bubble round this picture in your mind's eye . . . . Now
coming from various parts of your body there are what
appear to be strings attaching you to this thing you want . .
. . There may be many strings depending how strongly you
are attached to it . . . . Take a pair of scissors or a knife and
cut every single one of the strings . . . . Now you are going
to hand this bubble over to your highest self asking that it
comes to you only if and when it is in your highest good . . .
. Also ask your higher self that if any blocks stand in the
way of you receiving this thing, they be presented clearly so
that they can be processed and removed . . . . See that bubble float up and away . . . . Let go any expectations about
how this thing will be or when you will receive it . . . . Know
that if you don't have this thing now it is either because you
are not ready for it or it is not in your highest good . . . . Now
when you are ready bring your attention back into the room.

Try not to fixate or think too much about this thing as
this will only serve to reattach the strings. Let it go and get
on with your life.

EXPECTATIONS Versus EXPECTANCY

EXPECTATIONS ARE THE KEY TO DISAPPOINTMENT

Expectations and expectancy lead on from non-attachment. Expectations occur we go into a situation being set on a particular outcome. The things we expect rarely happen or when it does it does not give the desired effect, there is always an anticlimactic sense of disappointment. When we have an expectation of a particular outcome, we become so focused on that result that we often miss something even better that is presenting itself. For instance, if we went to a party with an expectation of attracting a particular member of the opposite sex, we then spend the evening trying to attract their attention and at the end of the party they leave with someone else. At that same party there may have been someone far better suited to us who we didn't notice trying to attract our attention because we were too busy watching our prey.

Expectancy on the other hand has a far more mystical, magical quality to it. It says "I know something really positive is going to emerge from this situation, person or thing but I don't know what it is and I am going to enjoy the unfolding process". When there is a sense of expectancy there is also an inherent positivity and lightness.

If we can start to approach each situation with an air of expectancy then this encourages us to start to learn to look for the positives in everything that happens. They are always there but often we get so fixated with what is wrong that we fail to notice what is right.

We often have expectations of people. Usually we expect people to behave just as we would. This rarely happens and can cause a great deal of discord within relationships. If we let go all expectations of people we are then able to accept them whatever they do and consequently we can have harmonious relationships.

With abundance it is important to begin to instil some expectancy and equally important to let go all expectations. If we know that we are going to be increasing our prosperity but have an expectation that it is going to come from winning the lottery, we then invest all our hopes and money on that one eventuality and when week after week our numbers fail to come up, disappointment and disillusionment set in and we give the whole process up in disgust. Meanwhile there were probably many opportunities being presented to us that were never acted upon.

Have an expectancy that our highest good is about to unfold but have no specific expectations as to how this may come about.

EXERCISE

1) Each day program:

I EXPECT AND AM OPEN TO RECEIVE MY HIGHEST GOOD THIS DAY.

LIMITLESSNESS

LIMITLESSNESS IS THE KEY TO MIRACLES

From the moment we are born we begin to have limitations put on us. We are told what we cannot do and hear the word "No" thousands of times in the first few years of life. Rarely are we told at any point in our development that we are limitless, powerful beings who can create anything that we can imagine. This is in fact the truth but we are not taught this and we are not given any role model to show us that it is even possible. There are no powers that have to be learned, we all have them already. One problem is that in the male dominated human race the left side of the brain has been in command, this is the logical side of the brain that will only deal with things that can be seen and proved. The right side of the brain that works with intuition, creativity, music, poetry and imagination has been given short shrift by the left brainies. They dismiss those working with the right brain as arty farty, eccentrics and weirdoes. Thus, supposedly putting them in their place as being insignificant in the "real" world. However, the key to our limitlessness dwells within our right brain and that is imagination.

The imagination is an extremely important tool in our quest to become limitless beings. Imagination is the doorway to higher realms and there is a very fine line between what is imagination and what could be our reality. I have always felt that children who have so called "imaginary friends" are in fact playing with little spirit children that they can see because they are working on a vibration that allows them to tap into higher realms. It is the imagination that allows them to do it. I always think it is wonderful when the parents go along with the child and incorporate the imaginary friend into their family life. This keeps the sense of limitlessness intact and does not make the child wrong.

The imagination is very much a muscle that needs to be used in order to stay in good nick. When I was a child, television was only an hour a day and the rest of the time my brother and I would spend reading or playing games that involved using the imagination. Reading is very good because it makes us create pictures in our mind out of the words that we read. Today many children's imaginations have atrophied because television, videos and computer games give them the images and don't allow them to create their own. Many parents have a struggle to get children to read books when the easy option is to just switch on the television.

Visualisations are a very good way to flex the imagination muscle. They work totally with the right brain and the unconscious mind changing patterns.

At this time we cannot even begin to imagine what is available to us in the limitless cosmos. This is an unfolding process. When we begin to open up and accept our limitless reality a new and vaster vista will open up to our view.

Miracles are a natural way of life for us and we will notice as we let go of the past and its limiting conditioning and open up to the higher vibrations, that miracles occur on a daily, hourly and even minutely basis. This is our normal state.

EXERCISES

1) Look at ways in which you limit yourself.
2) How do you keep yourself small?

3) What would you like to do but think you won't be good enough?

4) How do you limit the people you make yourself available to?

5) What would you like to do that you think is impossible?

6) Using you imagination start to push the boundaries of limitation.

7) Sit in a chair and take one topic from your list of what you think is impossible. This could be something like teleportation or instant manifestation.

8) Take five or ten minutes to imagine and visualise what that would be like. Enjoy the sensations and experience. Keep pushing the fantasy as far as your imagination can go.

GROUNDING AND MANIFESTATION

GROUNDING IS THE KEY TO EFFECTIVENESS

Manifestation is the process whereby we take the energy that has come from the Divine source and anchor it in the third dimension and this allows it to take a tangible form, whatever we choose that to be. It is like water. The higher the temperature the less dense it is. At a very high temperature it is invisible vapour, at a slightly lower temperature it can be seen as steam, then it becomes water and at the lowest temperature it is ice that is hard and dense, but it never actually changes its molecular structure. This is actually the same process with energy but instead of lowering the temperature we are lowering the vibrational frequency of that energy. As the frequency lowers, the energy will change its form, it will go through various stages of being pure light working down through the spectrum of colours and then becoming sound and gradually taking on tangible physical form. The denser the thing is the lower the vibration it is working with. In order to have the physical things in our lives we have to learn to convert this energy to the correct frequency and this requires that we ground that energy into the Earth and into the third dimension.

There is a strong tendency for those working in a spiritual way to be singularly ungrounded. We often do not want to work with our three base chakras and consequently become very top heavy and out of balance. It also means that we are only working with half the spectrum of colours. Red, orange and yellow tend to get omitted from our lives. These three base chakras deal with the physical and emotional bodies and if ignored they can begin to cause havoc in our lives. Our physical bodies will try and get our attention in a big way. They will either put on a great deal of weight or it may create some illness or discomfort. So many people tell me how they have put on weight since awakening spiritually without any change in their diet or habits. It is essential to start redressing the balance. Wear red, orange and yellow clothes, eat red, orange and yellow foods and take every opportunity to expose ourselves to red, orange and yellow light. We can take time to give our physical bodies some attention, there are many good physical therapies that can help. Try and connect with the ground as much as possible, stand on the grass with bare feet and send the energy focus down through the legs and into the ground. Those of us who are particularly ungrounded may need to do this regularly.

People who are noticeably ungrounded tend to live in their heads or in the higher realms. They look like they are on another planet and probably are. This is usually a form of escapism. When the human condition becomes too painful it seems to be an easier option but ultimately life has to shout louder in order to get us to learn our lessons. When we find that we are spending a great deal of time in our heads, we are probably either living in the past or the future and letting the present pass us by. In order to be in the now, we need to take our attention away from ourselves and observe what is going on around us. Something like juggling is marvellous for keeping us in the present because we have to concentrate and focus our attention on something outside of ourselves. There is only the here and now and if we are not experiencing it, we are letting life and opportunities pass us by.

Manifestation occurs when we have stepped down the energy to transform it into whatever form we choose to create. I believe that in the new order that manifestation is going to become the main tool for abundance. With manifestation products will not be created from the dwindling Earth's resources but come from the infinite source, and there will also be the ability to change one form into another when it has served its purpose. This probably sounds totally fantastical and too magical to be true and many of us possibly can't conceive how we could possibly achieve this end. The first part of the process is to let go any beliefs that it is impossible. If we believe it is, it will be. Open to the belief that we can create absolutely anything. Many people probably have experienced a form of manifestation without even knowing it. This occurs when we want something and without anyone knowing, we receive it as a present. We explain it as a coincidence. Another common scenario is when we are thinking about ringing someone we haven't spoken to for ages and the phone rings and it is them. This is our thoughts made manifest.

Manifestation comes quicker as we raise our own vibrational frequency for the higher the energy we have access to, the easier it all becomes. Visualisation and the imagination are an integral part of manifestation. If we see what we want in our mind's eye then we can bring that into physical form by grounding the energy into the correct frequency.

The balance of male and female, as we have already stated, is important to bring about manifestation, for it is the female side that receives the energy from source and then hands it over to the male that grounds the energy and brings about physical manifestation.

EXERCISES

1) Ground yourself every day.

2) Here are some methods.

a) Spend a few minutes outside each day. Feel the ground under your feet, connect with the Earth.

b) See a spherical ball of pure brilliant white light above your head. Bring it down right through your body and out through the soles of your feet and down into the centre of the Earth.

c) Visualise an anchor on a chain coming from the base chakra, lower it into the ground and then deeper into the Earth.

d) Visualise roots coming out of your feet and going deep into the ground.

e) Take your attention off yourself, observe what is going on around you. Notice nature and animals.

VISUALISATION

Before you start decide on something you would like to manifest into your life. It can be something material or else something like a job or a relationship. I would suggest you start with something that is attainable and then work up to more challenging feats as you become more confident.

Sit comfortably and relax . . . . Let everything go and take some deep breaths . . . . With every out breath you find yourself becoming more and more deeply relaxed . . . . High above you there is the infinite God source. You can see it as a huge pure brilliant white and gold orb . . . . It has no beginning and no end . . . . Focus for a few moments on it . . . . Out of this God source you see a cylinder of white light emerge and come down . . . . It goes right through the spectrum of rainbow colours from white to violet, from violet to indigo from indigo to blue to green to yellow to orange and red . . . . Then you begin to hear a very high thin sound . . . Gradually that sound becomes lower and lower as it goes through the whole spectrum of sound that is detectable by us . . . . When that sound is so deep that you can no longer hear it, focus just above your crown chakra, see a stage or platform where you are now going to visualise whatever it is that you want to manifest . . . . See it in as much detail as possible . . . . See it surrounded by a beautiful pink glow . . . . When you are satisfied that you have seen this thing just as you want it put a spotlight of white onto the picture and see the size of the picture getting smaller as the spotlight beam intensifies . . . . See it almost encapsulated by the beam . . . . When you have it down to the size of an orange see your female side receive it into the aura . . . . See it then coming down through the body from the crown chakra down through the head to the throat and down to the heart area . . . . At this point see your female side pass this orb of white light over to your male side knowing that he will ground it and know instinctively what to do in order to bring it into being. . . . See it continue its journey down through the solar plexus, the sacral area and then into the base chakra . . . . From here it continues deep into the ground . . . . Once you are sure that this visual picture has been grounded, allow your male and female sides to take this orb and together to let go of it and all attachment to it . . . . This will enable the thing to manifest in its right time and place without any interference from the self . . . . To finish off you are going to place a powerful magnet in your heart chakra . . . . Program this magnet to attract to you this thing you wish to manifest . . . . See the force field from this magnet intensifying first of all so that it encompasses the whole room you are in . . . . Then see it taking in the whole building . . . . Growing all the time to fill the village or town you are in . . . . Spreading rapidly to the whole country . . . . Then the whole world . . . . and finally the Universe . . . . Ask that if this thing be for your highest good that it manifest rapidly . . . . Also ask for any assistance you may need in order to receive it . . . . When you are ready bring your attention back into the room.

I would recommend doing this visualisation at least three times.

SPACE CLEARING

It has already been established that when there is a free flow of energy within our four body system, there is also a free flow of abundance energy in our lives. This, however, extends even further into our outer life. Our external life is merely a reflection of our internal selves. As we are clearing the inner blocks it is equally important to make sure that we are sorting out the things that represent what we are clearing. For instance, if we are working on letting go of an old relationship and clearing the emotional and mental baggage from that person, it is often necessary to clear some of the external baggage from that relationship. This baggage can be letters, cards or presents. A willingness to let these things go shows that we are also willing to let the relationship go. If we are not quite ready for this, it is important to be kind to ourselves and wait for the right moment.

Clutter is the main block to a free flow of energy. Anything that gathers dust and is not used or needed or has no aesthetic value should be sorted and discarded. I know that if I walk into a person's home that is very cluttered, I begin to feel very uncomfortable and often end up with a headache. Even if they have very beautiful things, I find I can't appreciate them because they are overwhelmed by the general clutter. Magazines are a classic example of things we hold onto and that block our energy. If we have not referred to them in the previous few months then the chances are that we never will. Bits of paper, old cards, receipts and paid bills all stack up and contribute to the clutter. File away what we need and discard what we don't.

There is an instant opportunity to increase our abundance by starting to clear our clutter. What is junk to us is another man's treasure. We can make substantial amounts of money by taking our clutter to a car boot sale. Anything left over can be dumped or contributed to someone else's car boot junk or given to a charity shop.

It is amazing how different our living and working space feels after we have cleared the clutter. It frees up our energy and allows us to tackle things that seemed overwhelming before.

For most of us there are draws or cupboards that we stuff things into that we don't particularly want to deal with or look at. Consequently, they become no go areas that we only open very quickly to stuff something else in. They can house some very old stuff like terse letters from the bank, income tax demands etc. There is often a great deal of negative energy surrounding these areas and sometimes a sense of foreboding at the thought of sorting through. It is important to have the courage to clear as much from these areas as possible and throw away or burn anything that does not relate to the present time. Each thing that we hold onto from the past that generates a bad feeling will continue to do so. We can make sure there are no areas in our homes or work place that we do not feel comfortable being near. If there is then it needs our immediate attention.

As I have already said, our homes are an outer representation of our inner selves and if there are drawers or cupboards or rooms in our home that we do not want to look at then there will also, almost certainly, be areas in our mental, emotional and physical bodies that reflect this totally. Often after trauma or bereavement we lock away memories and emotions that we feel we cannot deal with and those areas then become closed off to us. There is usually a great deal of fear attached to going in and clearing these areas, not knowing what might be uncovered. Some people never do look into them and sometimes these areas in the physical body will fester and create dis-ease in the body like cancer. As we have always stated, fear is always an illusion and if we have the courage to go in and sort it out, the reality is never as bad as the fear itself. The sense of relief and achievement afterwards is incredible. So be aware that if we have dark places in our homes that need clearing out, we probably also have some dark areas inside us that need some light directed onto them.

Feng Shui or the Chinese art of placement has become very popular in the West over the last ten years. Many businesses will call in consultants and take their advice very seriously. It takes into account the actual situation of the home or business and the good and bad indications that the location shows. Basically, the premise is that where Chi (life energy) is able to flow freely and unhindered then our lives work, however, there are many things that block the flow of chi and these things need to be rectified in order to restore the balance.

First of all the quality of the land is looked at. Whether there are hills, valleys, water, roads and what trees grow around. Do these things allow a good flow of chi to our home or business? Then the interior of the house is looked at by placing a Ba Gua over a plan of the house. A Ba Gua is an eight sided shape based on the I Ching. Each section of the Ba Gua relates to a different area of life experience and when placed over a plan of our homes that relate to that particular area of life. If that area is blocked in our homes, it is probably blocked in our lives. By making various changes we can unblock the flow of chi and see immediate shifts in our lives. The Ba Gua applies to the whole house and each room individually.

BA GUA

	Status	
Abundance		Relationships
Tribe	Centre	Creativity
Knowledge		Angels
	Life Path	

The Life Path line is placed over the front door or at the top of the stairs.

ABUNDANCE - Relates not just to money but to blessings and gifts from the Gods.

STATUS - Can be called the fame section. It relates your standing in the community. Whether you are high or low profile. Visible or invisible.

RELATIONSHIPS - Also sexuality. It relates to the base chakra and earth energy.

CREATIVITY - Can be relating to children and offspring. It is filled with fun, joy, it is clear and bright. If blocked creativity will have dried up.

ANGELS - Can be called helpful people. It relates to your support network or anyone who helps you.

LIFE PATH - This relates to your job or what you are contributing to the world. When clear, you make your living and enjoy it.

KNOWLEDGE - Inner wisdom. It stresses the need to BE in order to tap into universal wisdom. Needs to be calming and peaceful.

TRIBE - This relates to family and ancestors. It includes cultural traditions. Deals with residual issues from family members.

CENTRE - Where all points come together. Keep clear and balanced at all times. Affects health.

There is a tendency to repeat history in houses, even if the structure has been torn down and rebuilt. The energy remains in the land and it therefore needs to be consecrated.

Sometimes if an area of life is not working, the blockage can actually be in the area before. The flow of the energy is clockwise so if our abundance is not coming through the block may be in our tribal area. There may be family issues that need to be dealt with.

Even if our homes have a great many blockages, do not despair, there are things we can do to change this. Firstly, it is essential to remove the clutter as we have already stated.

Toilet lids should be left down, especially while flushing, to avoid an escape of chi down the drain.

Mirrors correct absent space. Convex mirrors deflect bad energy away.

Crystals concentrate energy and bring it into the space.

Plants encourage energy to rise up. Leaves should be rounded rather than spiky.

Heavy objects can anchor energy and can be put at the bottom of the stairs where stairs go straight into the front door.

Moving objects like wind chimes and mobiles change the quality of the energy.

Anything that makes sound like chimes or a flute or drum are very beneficial.

Fish tanks are good in the wealth area.

Where dogs sleep is good energy. Cats go for our negative energy.

Colour is a most important part of our home life. We often need more colour about to raise our energy levels.

This has just been a brief journey into Feng Shui. There are many good books available that go into more detail.

Geopathic stress is another area where we can be negatively affected in our home or work environment. It can be caused by proximity to power lines or underground environment issues like gasses or strong ley lines. It is identified by dowsing and can be localised to a foot or two.

Sometimes moving a bed or chair off a bad spot can have immediate and miraculous results to health and well-being. There are other remedies we can use like planting crystals but if it is totally chronic I would recommend moving.

EXERCISES

1) Clear clutter away from rooms.
2) Sort out cupboards and draws where you tend to put your personal effects.
3) I would recommend finding a basic book on Feng Shui and work on the rooms in your home.

POWER

Power and money are two words that are often put together. Personal power is not a concept that many people feel comfortable with and this is probably because the examples of people in power are rarely inspiring.

The mistake I think we make is confusing ego power with true Divine power. Since we see many instances of the former and virtually none of the latter I will endeavour to explain the difference between ego and Divine power as it appears to me. Ego power needs to feel that it is better that anyone else, it uses control and manipulation to keep others where it wants them. It uses fear to keep people in line and it sees the need to amass money or possessions or land in order to show people exactly how powerful it is. It is high profile and constantly needs to protect itself and its property from anyone who may want to destroy it or what belongs to it. It works on very masculine energy, it is always doing and has a great need to dominate, in relationships, in business, in politics, in every aspect of life. It gets its power through disempowering everyone else around them. Divine power, in contrast, uses the limitless universal energy in order to be, do and have whatever it chooses. It does not gain power by taking power or energy from others but actually makes power available to others. It allows everyone around it to make whatever choices they want because what they do does not in any way detract from it. It does not need to amass money or possessions because it knows it can manifest whatever it needs in any given moment. It knows that the best way to increase power is to empower those around it. It does not worry about anyone taking anything from it because it knows there is an endless supply and therefore it cannot detract from the source. It does not fear anything or anybody. It works with female energy that is the receiver from the source; it is nurturing and is more concerned with its being rather than its doing.

Perhaps the only role model who comes even close to the embodiment of Divine power is Jesus. So it is hardly surprising that we do not see that this power is readily available to absolutely all of us. Another reason that many people are unwilling to embrace power is that they have had lifetimes where they have abused power or else have witnessed first hand the abuse of power. The legacy of this is that there is a great deal of fear around the use of power. Again, I think this is due to the fact that the only image of power has been that of ego power.

When we begin to tap into and use our Divine power, abundance becomes the natural bi-product. I must make it clear that Divine power CANNOT be misused or abused. It can only work for the highest good of all mankind. We do not have to do anything to access this power, it is already there. We do, however, need to recognise that it exists and allow ourselves to use it. This is where the difficulty seems to lie. As I have stated earlier, if children witnessed their parents using this power and ability to manifest whatever they needed all the time, it would be the most natural thing in the world for a child or baby to follow suit without needing to develop any expertise. This is the ideal we need to aim for. If this seems too fantastical and impossible then it will be. The first step is to open our minds to the possibility and then take it from there. Our ego and logical mind will no doubt supply us with all the reasons why it could never happen and why we must be losing our marbles if we believe it can. If this happens, thank the mind and ego for voicing their opinion and carry on as if nothing has happened. When we ignore the ego it finds a way of making its presence felt, much as a child who is not given enough attention will often become naughty and obstreperous. Explain to the ego what we are doing, include it in our plans without actually giving in to its negative or limited thinking.

Apart from the spiritual powerful energy that we can tap into using our higher chakras, there is also a very powerful earth energy that we need to utilise. This is "prana" and it is accessed through our lower chakras. It is very important to have the balance of both these energies in order to function effectively and powerfully on the Earth.

The power centre in the body is the solar plexus. This is an area where many people feel a strong vulnerability. This area also works with the emotions and through thousands of years of male conditioning we are made to believe that emotions are a weakness that should be suppressed. The very opposite is in fact true. It is no coincidence that the power and emotions dwell in the same area of the body, it is our emotional body that sets us apart from many other species both on Earth and in the rest of the Universe. It is essential that we begin to change our perceptions about where our strengths and weaknesses lie. We are often very protective of our solar plexus area. If people are feeling unsure of themselves they will often cover this area over with their arms or clothes. This is where we feel our vulnerability is located. Our vulnerability is what makes us strong not weak. It is a very powerful force and as such has its own protection built in. There is a saying in the Course in Miracles, "My safety lies in my defencelessness". I take this to mean that if we feel the need to defend something it is broadcasting to the world to attack. However, if something cannot be hurt or destroyed then there is no need to protect it. If we are not defending our power, our emotions and our vulnerability out of fear then no one is going to try and attack us. Hence these things have no need of a protective mechanism. It is like a house with an alarm system, close circuit TV, armed guards and killer dogs. This is broadcasting to the world that there is something valuable inside and therefore it would become a target. Whereas a house with all its doors and windows open and a visitors welcome sign would indicate that there would not be anything that anyone could take from it. So which house is safer?

It is important that we begin to familiarise ourselves with our personal power. Try it on for size and begin to flex our power muscle in slow degrees waiting until we feel comfortable before moving onto the next level. This way we can integrate it gently into our every day life.

EXERCISES

1) Write a list of qualities you think activating your personal power would give you.
2) As you write this list notice what comes up.

a) Do you feel fear?

b) Do you feel excitement?

c) Do you feel resistance?

d) Does a voice tell you these things are impossible?

e) Do you wonder what you need to do to GET these things?

f) Do you see it as a burden or responsibility?

3) CRUD any fear or negative beliefs that emerge from this exercise.

VISUALISATION

Power is not something that we need to obtain. We already have it, we just have to remove the dark veils of illusion that obscure it from us. This visualisation is designed to begin this process.

Sit comfortably and start to take some deep breaths . . . . Let everything go . . . . With every breath you become more deeply relaxed . . . . You are going to go on an internal journey to your seat of power . . . . Focus your attention on your inner self and begin to travel from your head area down inside your body, past your liver and your lungs and spleen . . . . until you reach your solar plexus area . . . . You see a door in front of you marked POWER . . . .This is the seat of power in your physical body . . . . There may be just one door separating you from your power or there may be many with other obstacles in the way . . . . Open this first door and see if you gain admittance to your power. You know when you have reached it because you will almost be blinded by the strength of the pure brilliant white light that you see . . . . If there are other doors or things in the way, open or remove them now . . . . Go into this beautiful power light, acclimatise yourself to it . . . . Allow yourself to feel comfortable with it . . . . Feel it merging with you so that you no longer feel separate from it . . . . Does it give you a sense of joy and bliss? . . . . Take it all in . . . . If you choose, this could become your natural state . . . . There is no need to protect it because it cannot be touched . . . . When you feel totally at one with that wonderful energy you can come away from that place . . . . See that any doors or obstacles that were there before have just dissolved away . . . . Return past those vital organs again and when you are in your head area, switch your attention from your inner self to your outer self . . . . Look at your solar plexus and see if you can see that beautiful light of your power self . . . . The chances are that you either cannot see it or it is dim. This is because of the veils of illusion separating you from this power . . . . These veils will appear to be like suits of clothes or cloaks that you are wearing . . . . Start to take off these clothes now . . . . Each layer represents some illusions that you have bought into over your life time . . . . Some layers will be fear, some will be beliefs that you are not good enough, some will be belief in your separation from God. . . . You do not need to know precisely what the cause of each layer is, just shed it . . . . You may begin to notice as you take more layers off that you can see the light shining through the other layers . . . . As more veils are removed, that light becomes brighter and brighter . . . . See all the clothes you have taken off being burnt up by the purple flames of transmutation . . . . As the last few layers come off you can see and feel your whole body glowing strongly in a huge aura around you . . . . This is your natural state . . . . This is who you are . . . .Once again know that it is its own protection. You are completely safe . . . . There is no responsibility, you only need to BE to utilise this power . . . . Bask in this energy for a while and when you are ready bring your attention back into the room.

RECEIVING

Receiving is a conscious choice that we need to make in order to have an abundant life. It is not automatic as many might expect. If we are not living abundantly it is not because the gift has not been given, it is because it has not been received.

Our Divine selves wants us to be plentiful and joyful and fulfilled. It does not withhold these things until we have learned a lesson or until we have reached a certain level of enlightenment. These things are available to every single person on the planet, regardless of who they are or what they have done.

It is necessary for us to know that the gift has been given in order that we can then choose to receive it. Many people go through life waiting for the bad news and because they are looking for it they always find it. A slight change in perception can allow one instead of expecting and receiving the bad news to receive the good. If we expect to have miracles then we almost certainly will have them.

There are many reasons why people have a problem with receiving. Some of these we have covered. Feeling that we don't deserve it, fear that it is greedy to have when others do not. Belief that in order to serve, we need to denounce any material gain. Belief in lack and a sense of guilt at having more than our fair share and many others.

We need to look at our responses to receiving. When we are given a present, what is the reaction? Do we feel embarrassed that someone has taken the time and trouble to give us something? Do we mentally assess the cost of the gift and try to decide if the person has spent more than they can easily afford? Do we try and think of a way to pay the person back as soon as possible? Do we feel guilty? Do we wonder if there is an ulterior motive to the gift? Do we accept it with joy and pleasure? Do we plan to take it back and swap it for something we like better? Do we try and think who we could give it to that might like it? Examine the response we would have to being given, perhaps a surprise gift. This is probably the same response that we unconsciously give to the offer of a gift from the Universe.

In my experience, people who give all the time have a big problem with receiving. It is almost as if the giving is there to camouflage this. Giving is often a way of trying to buy love, but the person is probably not able to receive the love even if it is given freely. This becomes a vicious circle whereby the person tries harder to buy affection and then feels cheated at not getting a very good return on their money.

The Universe is a perfect mirror; it will send back to us what we send out. Even if we decide that we are open to receive but if we are coming from a position of lack or desperation, the Universe will send back that lack and despair and that is what we will end up receiving.

It is important that we do not have any explicit expectations as to what we will receive as we rarely create exactly what we expect and consequently there is often disappointment.

It seems to me that the receiving mechanism is one of a balanced flow between giving and receiving. If we start the flow by giving while at the same time allowing the receiving channel to be open for energy to flow freely. Giving should always be totally unconditional and the receiving should be done with joy and gratitude. When we have this mechanism balanced we will notice a change in our fortunes. It is important to notice that this giving and receiving is often not material. It can be time, energy, love, healing, thoughts or information. We will often receive from a totally different source and in a different form from the ones that we have given, so try not to balance the books in a literal sense.

EXERCISES

1) Make a list of your responses to receiving a gift.

2) Do you push away offers of help?

a) Do you allow yourself to enjoy what you are given?

b) Do you immediately find ways to repay the gift?

c) Do you feel manipulated by gifts, etc.?

4) Look at your responses and note that if you have a problem with receiving gifts you will also have a problem with receiving the bounty that the Universe is offering you.

5) Take some time to open up your receiving channels. Sit or stand and begin to take some very deep breaths, the breath represents you taking in the life force. At a point at the back of the neck see a channel opening up and then see some pure white light from the God source, entering into your body and filling it with this beautiful energy. Take a few minutes to fully receive this energy.

6) Finally stand with feet apart and your arms open wide and say three times.

I OPEN MYSELF TO RECEIVE MY HIGHEST GOOD.

BREAKING PATTERNS

BREAKING PATTERNS IS THE KEY TO GETTING OUT OF A RUT

One of the strangest human traits is that of repeating behaviour time after time and getting the same negative response. We all do it hoping that this next time the outcome will be different. We get stuck in a groove and yet try using the same method to get out of it that has failed time and time again.

This manifests for some people in relationships, where in the pursuit of true love, they attract alcoholics or in some way emotionally dysfunctional partners again and again.

Often our patterning has been set in very early childhood and most of our patterns are totally unconscious. It is therefore quite difficult to change something that we don't even know we are doing. Patterns occur so that we can clear the origin of that pattern that often has some trauma or unresolved feelings or beliefs attached to it. As a child I had a pattern of getting lost in public places, like St. Marks Square in Venice, Marks and Spencers and a crowded beach in Cornwall. When I went back to the first time I ever got lost, I was eighteen months old and my mother was away and I just walked out of the garden gate to try and find her. Obviously there was a great deal of emotion around the incident that my unconscious was trying to resolve.

Patterns appear in every area of our lives. Work, relationships, family, in our social lives, where we spend our holidays and in our home. In order to start breaking them we need to first identify them. If something happens once, then we can dismiss it as an isolated incident, if it happens twice then it needs to be looked at and if it happens three or more times then it is firmly established and needs immediate attention. I have a client who had a pattern whereby he was always being robbed and pilfered by his own employees. In spite of two businesses failing with considerable loss to him, he had not recognised this pattern and had just started up a new business with a partner. That very day they had set up new bank accounts for the business and it turned out that the bank would not allow the partner to be a single signatory for any of the accounts as he had been involved with ventures before, which had had financial irregularities, a fact my client was totally ignorant of. Fortunately the bank managed to safeguard a further repeat of that pattern in this instance. We discovered that the source of this pattern went back to his childhood where some of the servants employed in his home had taken liberties.

Some of our patterns are harmless. These can be things like how we get ready for bed or the route we take to work or what we eat for breakfast. Sometimes in order to shake up the unconscious a bit it is a good idea to vary this behaviour. This stops us being quite such a robot. It can also add variety and spice to our relationships and the mundane things we have to do in life. Predictability and boredom can destroy a relationship.

We all have patterns of behaviour regarding money and unless we identify and change them they can have a detrimental affect on our lives. Some people have a debt pattern, so that no matter how much money they have coming in, they will spend until they are in the red. Very often the things they spend the money on they neither need nor want, they will sit in drawers or wardrobes untouched. This person is reacting to a compulsion to spend. There will always be a root cause for this behaviour that needs to be identified. Other people are compulsive savers, no matter how much money they have and how much they might need an item they find themselves unable to buy it. We all have money patterns that are not quite as extreme as these but they will be running us just the same. We can look at our patterning concerning paying bills, do we send them off straight away or wait for the final, final demand? Do we view bills with a sense of dread or are they like any other mail. If this patterning is causing any sort of negative response, we can change it by paying by direct debit or changing to a key system where we buy our electricity or gas in advance.

EXERCISES

Look at and change your patterns in the following ways:

1) Identify what the pattern is. For this you only need to open your eyes and look at your life.

2) Try and find out the origin of this pattern and clear any emotions and beliefs that have been created from it. If this is hard try and trace the pattern back to the first one you can remember. Discuss it with a friend, member of the family or counsellor. They can often see your life more clearly than you can.

3) Notice when you have just unknowingly repeated the pattern. DO NOT give yourself a hard time for this, instead give yourself a pat on the back for having recognised it.

4) Catch yourself while in the middle of repeating that pattern. Change your behaviour at this stage if you still can. If not, then just observe how the rest of the scenario unfolds.

5) Realise just before you are about to start on that pattern of behaviour and decide to react differently. You may have to repeat this stage quite a few times before you completely break out of this pattern.

6) Remain **CONSCIOUS** at all times. Patterns work on an unconscious level.

7) Some of our patterns are good and work positively for us. "If it ain't broke, don't fix it."

8) Look at your patterns concerning money. Write them down. This includes:

Your relationship with the bank.

The way you pay and react to bills.

Do you work with cash, cheques or credit?

Do you buy things you don't want?

Do you not buy things you need?

Are you generous or tight with your money?

Do you feel guilty if you spend money?

Do you always look for a bargain?

9) Trace these patterns back to origin. Were they created from following or reacting against family problems?

10) Make a list of ways in which you can begin to break those patterns that are negative.

GIVING

Giving is the other side of the coin from receiving and both need to be in balance in order to allow abundance energy to flow freely.

When we have got our chalice of abundance working so that energy is always immediately replenished from source and no matter how much we use it cannot be depleted, then giving will be something that is done on a large scale. It is only when we think that there will not be enough for ourselves to manage on that we curb our giving. Once this belief is removed and there is complete trust that we have an endless supply that cannot be diminished then the world will change dramatically. We can see that if only one person totally worked with this principle then poverty could totally be abolished on the planet.

Giving is not just about money or material goods. It is often time, expertise, advice, information, joy, laughter and love. As we move forward into the new order these are the things that will hold the most value. It is very important that we are plugged into the energy source so that our own energy does not become depleted and we go into burnout mode. This has happened to many people and often what happens is that the body's immune system packs up and the person ends up catching bugs and viruses that they cannot shake off easily. So we can make sure we are plugged in before giving into endless demands on our energy. Getting plugged in may be a gradual process whereby at sometime we can be totally energised and can stand giving plenty away and other times we may have inadvertently cut off from source and therefore be a bit more sparing with our own energy. We just need to be able to tune into ourselves and check out the state of our electrics.

Giving needs to be unconditional. If we have the need for thanks and gratitude then it is not unconditional. Let go any expectations of any reaction. Any positive response is therefore a bonus. If we have a bit of a problem with this, try an experiment with anonymous giving. If it is a gift of money, make sure it is cash or a money order. We don't want to leave any clues for them to identify us by, use a different postmark if sending it and disguise the writing or type any accompanying words. We can notice how this makes us feel. Whenever we give we will also receive but rarely from exactly the same source and when we do get a return from someone it will often not be in the same form that we gave it to them.

Tithing is an old form of giving. Basically, we are meant to tithe ten percent of our available income, giving it away to those who are needier than us. These days I think they call it income tax and the percentage is much higher.

When we give we need to make sure that we have no ulterior motives. It may be to buy friendship, to impress someone, to put someone off balance, out of a sense of duty or guilt, in order to feel superior or any other reason. In these cases the ego is at work and the giving is not from our Divine selves. The other person will sense this whether consciously or unconsciously and therefore their reaction at receiving the gift may be less positive than it would otherwise be and inevitably that negativity will come back to us. What we put out we will get back.

EXERCISES

1) Find one or more opportunities to practice anonymous giving. It may be to a friend or even someone you don't know. It may be paying the parking charge or toll for the car behind you, or do a kind act for someone you have never met before without waiting for the thanks. It could be sending a present in the mail to a friend but not on a birthday as it is more impactful that way. Or send an anonymous gift of money to someone you know is hard up.

2) Check out how this feels.

HEAVEN ON EARTH

Our collective purposes in this lifetime is to co-create Heaven on Earth. This is not just a pie in the sky concept. It is now well within our grasp.

We are all extremely fortunate to live on such a beautiful planet. It is completely fruitful and abundant and yet we have done our best to try and destroy it over the last few thousand years.

Religions have always represented Heaven as a place that we go to after death and only if we have been good and kept to their rules. Heaven is everywhere and Heaven is also a state of mind. Two people could be leading parallel lives. To all intents and purposes the various factors of their lives could be the same and yet one could be in Heaven and the other in Hell. How we choose to perceive our lives and surroundings is how they will be. Heaven does not depend on any external factors, it does not matter how much money we have, whether we are in a good relationship or what job we have. It only depends on how we choose to feel inside. What level of peace, contentment and happiness we choose to have. Happiness is a decision, it does not come about as a result of certain things that happen to us. Some people will be happy no matter what their lot, others are miserable in spite of seeming to have everything.

So how do we reach this wonderful state of mind? First of all we need to give up any thoughts or beliefs that something or someone will make us happy. We are the only people who can make us happy. We all indulge in the "I'll be happy when..." syndrome. We look at our lives and see what seems to be less than perfect and then we fixate on our need to have or do these things and we convince ourselves that only if we had that we would be perfectly content. More often than not if we do manage to reach that goal we are surprised at how empty we feel and how our life has changed very little. We then fixate on something else.

Acceptance is the key to happiness. If we can learn to accept that in any given moment our lives are perfect, just as they are. Any shortcomings in our lives are there because we have chosen those particular challenges in this lifetime in order to learn and grow. If we can see these challenges as being something positive and not negative and that we have chosen the gifts and talents needed to work through them. If we can just change our perception and accept these circumstances as they are, we stop fighting against them all the time and we are able to move on from them more quickly. This acceptance frees us totally and allows us to face each day with eager anticipation and not a sense of dread or impending doom. We know we have reached this wonderful state when we can feel happy every day without having a reason for it. At this point because we are sending out such positive vibrations we attract to us positive loving people and wonderful miracles and situations and bingo, we have achieved Heaven on Earth.

Hell on Earth works exactly the same but in reverse. If we send out fearful thoughts we will attract negative people and situations and this only serves to reinforce the belief that it's a bad world and everyone is out to get us. We then get into a downward spiral that can be very difficult to pull ourselves out of.

In order to change our lives, we have only to change our minds.

EXERCISES

1) Look at your life now. On a scale of 1 - 100 to what degree have you achieved Heaven on Earth?

2) Write a list of what will supposedly make you happy.

e.g. I'll be happy when I'm in a wonderful relationship.

I'll be happy when I'm thin.

I'll be happy when I'm rich, etc.

3) Then release these by writing out three times:

I release the belief that I'll be happy when . . . . . . then burn it.

4) Look at ways in which you can accept and incorporate these shortcomings into your life.

5) Choose to be happy with who and what you are.

6) Each day: Make a decision to be happy, no matter what life throws at you.

7) Everything that happens is just as it should be.

8) Check in as to whether there is a message or lesson you need to take from each situation, thank it and then let it go.

KARMA

RELEASE IS THE KEY TO LEAVING THE PAST BEHIND

One of the blocks to abundance and prosperity on a spiritual level is karma. In all our many life times we may have experienced extreme wealth and extreme poverty; we will have taken from these experiences varying attitudes to money and abundance. We then take these attitudes with us into future lives unless we manage to clear them within that lifetime. For instance, if we had a lifetime where we had abused or witnessed the abuse of money, this would affect our response to having money in other lifetimes.

When we are born we choose our parents and we also choose various factors of our lives to come, like religion, race and wealth. We choose these things in order to provide us with the necessary challenges in order to learn, grow and clear karma. This, however, does not mean that we are stuck with that situation for the whole of that lifetime. As soon as we have learned the lessons those circumstances were there to create and let go of any residue from it, we are able to create whatever we want.

We can begin to be aware of what aspects of our attitudes to money come from previous lives when we start clearing our mental beliefs. We start to see that certain situations in our lives cannot be explained by mental beliefs alone. We do not have to live out our karma anymore, we simply have to choose to consciously let it go.

While writing this book I visited my parents in Bermuda and while I was out there did quite a few sessions for people on the island. What struck me forcibly was that lack of money or fear or worry about money did not come up as an issue for any of these people, in spite of the fact that some were in fairly low paid jobs. Whereas in England it has virtually come up for every client I have ever seen, regardless of what standard of living they were enjoying. I mentioned this to some friends, a couple of whom had travelled extensively and another who was from South America and had lived all over the world. They all agreed that when they were in other countries they hardly thought or worried about money but as soon as they stepped off the plane in Britain they were consumed by a sense of lack and worry about surviving financially. This was corroborated by many other people that led me to surmise that there was a karma attached to the country involving money and wealth. This karma related to Empire days when Britain invaded so many areas of the planet with a view to taking all valuable resources from those countries. What goes around comes around and I feel that the country is now paying the price for that greed and domination. However, as I have already stated, we have only to let go of karma once we are aware of it. Using similar techniques I would use on an individual I worked with a group to clear this karma. This fear over money has become such a habit that we need to consciously decide not to do it anymore. It is up to each individual as to whether they let go of their own personal attachment to it.

It will be very helpful for many of us to identify our past lives that may be blocking abundance and prosperity in this life. This can be done by ourselves or with the help of someone who works with past lives.

EXERCISES

1) Look at the set of circumstances that you chose to be born into.

2) Find clues as to what lessons you were meant to learn from those circumstances.

3) Look at whether those lessons have been learned or at what you still need to do.

4) Find out as many past lives blocking abundance as possible.

5) Say this affirmation:

I RELEASE ALL KARMIC DEBT CONCERNING ABUNDANCE AND PROSPERITY.

DEBT

For some people reading this book debt may be a very real issue. So we will look at the mechanics of it on many levels.

On a mental level debt occurs when our negative thoughts and beliefs about money outweigh the positive ones. This may seem hard to combat because when we find ourselves in that situation we are almost constantly worrying and each of these worrying thoughts only pushes us further into the negative. The first thing to do is to start to illuminate the worrying thoughts. Distract the mind by doing something else that requires our full attention, or do an affirmation mantra mentioned in the magnetism chapter. Next look at the situation objectively and see what lesson or message we are meant to receive from it. We can then do whatever we need to show the Universe that this lesson has been learned. Then start to bring in trust. Trust is the very thing that can abolish the worry.

When we are in debt, usually large amounts of fear are generated. This fear will often feed off itself until it reaches gargantuan proportions. We may fear the bank manager who may appear to be an ogre. We may fear the postman because every time those letters plop on the mat there may be further demands for money. This fear becomes so destructive because it often prevents us from doing what we need to do to get ourselves out of the situation. It can paralyse us to the extent that it makes the situation even worse, we stick our heads in the sand and hope it will all go away. We put any nasty looking letters in the drawer unopened and we may even go out and buy something to cheer ourselves up. Fear can create what we fear most because we are giving so much time, energy and thought to it. In order to deal with fear, it is necessary to first of all recognise and acknowledge exactly what it is that we are afraid of. Often we feel fear without having a clue why. Once we have identified the cause of the fear, it is then about facing it and seeing what we may need to do. For this it is really important that we get support. Some of this support may be from friends who may be able to give us moral support. It may also necessary to get professional support. There are quite a few organisations there to help us deal with debt and they need not cost anything. They will not judge us or treat us like a child but will give practical advice on how to deal with our creditors.

If our fear of debt is not founded in reality then it is necessary to deal with the fear as an illusion which is what it is. Bring the fear into the light and see it disappear.

I honestly believe that for every problem there is a perfect solution and this solution is ideal for everyone involved. However, when we are feeling powerless and victimised by circumstances we sometimes forget to look for the solution, but it is always there and the clues are there as well. When we find ourselves in a difficult situation it is important not to allow ourselves to feel helpless and hopeless and sorry for ourselves but instead to change our perception and see it as a puzzle that needs solving and that finding that solution could even be enjoyable and very satisfying.

Look at various ways that we can make some extra money to help clear our debts. It could be by doing a car boot sale, doing something creative and selling it, or it may be baby-sitting or bar work. There are many other possibilities that we could explore. Perhaps get some friends over for a brainstorming session.

EXERCISES

1) Find out the full extent of your debt.

2) Put all your creditors on a list in order of importance. Make sure you put those that are charging interest near the top of the list.

3) Contact your creditors affirming your willingness to pay them and perhaps setting up a payment plan of so much per week or month. Do not promise to pay back more than you can afford as this will recreate the problem.

4) GET SUPPORT.

5) Make a list of ways in which you can make extra money.

6) Make moves to start putting these ideas into action, e.g, if you are doing a car boot sale, start sorting through your junk.

7) Do a visualisation and manifestation seeing all your bills marked **PAID**.

BREATH, LOVE AND PROSPERITY

Breathing is something we take totally for granted. Usually we are not at all conscious of our breath and while most people acknowledge that it is breath that gives us life, that is probably as far as it goes.

The depth of the breath sends messages to the brain that determines how we feel and react to situations. If we only breathe shallowly, the resulting brain waves set up a fight or flight mechanism in the body. It says that there is some danger at hand and the body produces adrenaline in order to cope with the impending danger and there is a feeling of fear. This is all very well when there is a situation to be fearful of but most of the time there is no such thing so the person will often find something to be afraid of in the set of circumstances they find themselves in and this thing will trigger further panic attacks, thus reinforcing the fear.

Beta brain waves occur with slightly deeper breath. This state occurs during the normal active periods of the day. Delta waves come with a state of relaxation and the breath is slower and deeper. We feel more content and at one with ourselves. Some people find it hard to reach even this state while awake. Even when they are supposedly relaxing they are uptight and needing to do something, this is because they are not allowing the breath to deepen. There is an even deeper state that occurs when the body is completely relaxed. The breath is very deep and slow. Experienced meditators can reach this state consciously by using the breath. For most people it is like the feeling we get just before we fall asleep. This state allows the body to heal itself more effectively and the brain waves have slowed to such an extent that the incessant mind chatter that we experience virtually disappears. Some people can experience feelings of bliss or ecstasy in this state.

So this is the choice of states that is available to us at any one time from fear and panic to ecstasy, governed only by the depth of our breathing. There is an unlimited amount of air available to us and yet many people are choosing not to use it and to stay stuck in the panic and fear.

Equally there is an unlimited source of abundance available to us just for the taking and yet most people are choosing to stay stuck in struggle and lack. When we become aware of this, it seems ridiculous. I believe that there is a strong correlation between the amount of breath we take in and the amount of abundance we allow into our lives. Therefore, if we consciously choose to breathe more fully we allow ourselves to feel better and happier and we then allow more abundant energy into our lives and bodies.

I also think that this correlation extends to love. I think there is a definite connection between the amount of love energy we allow into our lives and the amount of abundance energy. We are not talking here about the amount that we are loved but the degree of it that we let in. I have had clients whose partners and family love them very dearly but they are constantly rebuffing a large part of that love, feeling unworthy to accept it. So as with the breath it is not a lack of availability that is the issue but a lack of acceptance. Breath, love and abundance are all just energy in different forms, if we accept one we accept all and if we reject one we reject all.

EXERCISES

BREATH

1) Try to become more conscious of your breathing and whenever you think about it take more deep breaths. A very deep breath should inflate the stomach without the shoulders or the upper chest moving at all.

2) Take five or ten minutes a day sitting quietly with your eyes closed breathing very slowly and deeply.

3) If you are feeling stressed, uptight or panicky, stop and breathe deeply.

LOVE

1) Look at areas in your life where you do not let love in.

2) Be conscious of how you deflect love away from you.

3) Start changing these patterns.

16 Tips for Abundance

1. SEE THE DIVINE AS THE SOURCE.
2. ASK FOR WHAT YOU WANT. Always add the proviso that it be for your highest good.
3. TRUST, TRUST, TRUST. Trust will always abolish worry and fear.
4. BANISH ANY SENSE OF LACK.
5. YOUR NATURAL STATE IS TO BE WEALTHY.
6. PROSPERITY IS THE EFFECT, YOU ARE THE CAUSE. When abundance begins to arrive do not focus on the money, focus on the source.
7. STOP TRYING TOO HARD. THIS IS A LETTING GO PROCESS.
8. LET GO ALL EXPECTATIONS. If you see money coming from a particular place you block it.
9. REMEMBER TO BE GRATEFUL AND GIVE THANKS FOR WHAT YOU HAVE.
10. SURRENDER.
11. LISTEN FOR GUIDANCE.
12. THERE IS ONLY NOW. Don't see your prosperity coming from the future.
13. PLAN TO MEET EVERY NEED WITH PLENTY TO SPARE AND SHARE.
14. ALLOW YOURSELF TO RECEIVE AND ACCEPT YOUR ABUNDANT STATE.
15. DON'T FORGET TO BREATHE.
16. LOVE IS ALL.

Mental Beliefs

The following pages contain examples of mental beliefs to help give ideas and to supplement your own.

General Beliefs About Money

Money is a worry.

Money is there to be spent.

You should only buy what you can afford.

If you work hard you have more to spend.

You need to save for a rainy day.

Rich people get their money by being selfish and uncaring.

People with money are showy.

Money is limited.

Only a few people can have all the money they want.

A large proportion of our money goes on taxes.

Having money creates jealousy in others.

It takes so much to protect your money and possessions when you have it.

Having money is a measure of success.

Money can ruin friendships.

If you enjoy your work it doesn't bring in money.

Money is an ego power.

Money can only be obtained by manipulation.

Money is the root of all evil

Money does not grow on trees.

Personal Beliefs About Money

I have to wait until next month when there will be more.

I can't make money by doing something I enjoy.

If I work hard I have more to spend.

If I want something I will buy it if I possibly can.

When I put it on Visa I don't have to pay for it.

My child has all that he wants.

A holiday costs so much money.

There are lovely things that I want but can't afford.

There is never enough for what I want.

I don't deserve to be rich.

I don't deserve to have money spent on me.

Money is not important when I have it.

Money is very important when I don't have any.

Dad will always bail me out if I need it.

Clothes are so expensive.

Money is always spent recklessly.

I hate asking for money.

Money breaks up the family.

Women and Money

As a woman you always depend on others for money.

A fat wallet makes a man more attractive.

A woman never gets paid her worth.

If you are a mother and work, something will suffer.

A woman will give up her standard of living if she leaves
her relationship.

A woman's security is dependant on a man.

Women are useless with money.

A woman needs a man to take care of her.

A woman's place is in the home.

A woman needs a man to give her security.

A woman needs a man's pension to be secure in her future.

Men control money.

Men and Money

Men are supposed to support their family.

The meaning of life is to pay your bills.

A mortgage is a life sentence.

A man's main focus is his work.

Money is the man's department.

Men make money, women spend it.

A man's self worth is tied up with his job.

The more money you have, the more attractive women you
can expect to have.

Women drain your energy.

A family costs a fortune.

A man is needed to be the bread winner.

Women are only interested in a meal ticket.

Society's Beliefs About Money

If you have no job you are a drain on society.

If you are bankrupt you are a second class citizen.

There is not enough to go round.

Money is evil.

Having money is evil.

Money is the root of all evil.

You have to have a pension.

You have to have a mortgage.

You have to have stocks and shares.

Living is expensive.

You should be able to look after yourself.

You must have an insurance policy.

Life is to work hard.

Having money causes jealousy.

Money is power.

Success is measured by what you have and not who you are.

You can never be too rich or too thin.

Without qualifications you can't earn good money.

Men should be paid better than women.

If you want to make money you have to work hard and
    earn it.

It takes money to make money.

The filthy rich are usually crooks or exploiters.

If you work in the caring professions you can't expect to
    earn much.

If you are a single mother you will be on the breadline.

If you have more money than you need you are greedy.

If you have money people won't like you.

Money and Spirituality

Money and spirit are incompatible.

If I choose a spiritual path, I give up any aspirations to wealth.

A spiritual life involves poverty and struggle.

I can't charge for healing.

Money is evil.

If I am spiritual I must detach from the material world.

Suffering is character building.

If I love what I do I shouldn't expect to be paid for it.

God expects me to be poor.

Anyone with money is in collusion with the devil.

I should share and give freely of everything I have.

It is selfish and greedy to want things when others are starving in the world.

Money does not bring me happiness.

Wanting material things keeps me away from my spirit.

Spirituality is connected with money.

Fears About Having Money

I'll become greedy.

My life will be superficial.

I won't be able to do my spiritual work.

I might become vain.

Men wouldn't want me to have more money than them.

I'll be imprisoned in my fortress to preserve my goods.

People might only want me to be friends for my money.

People will envy me.

I could get used to a better life style and then lose it.

The responsibility and red tape that money involves.

An invasion of privacy by institutions and government.

All my time and energy taken up with managing and distributing my money.

I'm afraid of being called a rich bitch.

I'll have to socialise more and be more visible.

Fears About Not Having Money

I'm not free.

I am tied to a job I hate.

I am always worried about paying bills.

I won't have a roof over my head.

I can't travel.

I can't enjoy myself.

I could be cold.

I can't buy nice things.

I can't pursue creative, fulfilling activities.

I can't buy presents for others.

There is no happiness.

I feel sorry for myself.

I might miss out on something.

Liz Adamson is available for talks, workshops and intensive 3 hour one to one sessions.

Contact: Flat 3, Hamptons, Hadlow, Tonbridge, Kent, TN11 9SR. Tel 07940 101918. Email liz@edenbook.co.uk

Also available by Liz Adamson

The 12 Principles of Optimal Living	£7.95
Relationships, A Journey into Wholeness	£7.95
Abundance and Prosperity.	£7.95

The Ultimate Guides to Emotional Freedom

Releasing Anger	£4.95
Releasing Hurt and Sadness	£4.95
Embracing Love	£4.95
Embracing Happiness	£4.95

The Secrets of Optimal Living inspiration cards £7.95

All above titles soon available on high quality CDs

Available from Diviniti Publishing. Tel 01732 220373 Website: www.hypnosisaudio.com

Also available from Diviniti Publishing best selling hypnosis tapes and CDs including:

Complete Relaxation

Lose Weight Now

Heal Your Body and many others.